"John Tchicai brought a peace and intellect into the world of music at a time when righteous anger defined so much of the energy. John understood the power of love and transposed it through his work and his life. If anyone can relay the story and the message of the messenger of peace it would be his dear heart Margriet. This book is both biography and missive, an embrace of the true essence of music, be it jazz or opera - to heal and to reveal." - Thurston Moore, Sonic Youth

"I had to listen to John Tchicai for a while before I HEARD him... and once I HEARD him, his music changed my life! John had a keen ear for tone and timbre and possessed a highly fluid rhythmic concept: he could build an improvisation with the rigor of a composer and write compositions that catapult the improviser into fresh territory. Tchicai was a complete artist and we can all learn much from his legacy of compositions and recordings." - Charlie Kohlhase, saxophonist/composer, professor at the Longy School of Music at Bard College, Cambridge, MA

"John had a lot of fun in his life, I think there was a lot of humor in his way of looking at things. I mean serious humor, they sort of went hand in hand." - Bent Clausen, vibraphonist

"I always felt John was a very gentle soul, that wanted the best from everyone so they could grow. He was a deep, heavy, beautiful cat, that I had so much respect and love for. I'm so fortunate to have met you two. Your book will give John's life a wonderful, meaningful sense of order." - Russ Tucker, schoolteacher/jazz fan, Davis, CA

John Tchicai

A chaos with some kind of order

Margriet Naber

Ear Mind Heart Media

CONTENTS

CONTENTS

To Julie Tchikai Iversen and Yolo Tchicai

Published by Ear Mind Heart Media, Nijmegen, The Netherlands
First Printing, 2021

ISBN 978-90-831471-0-9
NUR 661

BIO004000 BIOGRAPHY & AUTOBIOGRAPHY / Music
MUS022000 MUSIC / Instructions & Study / General
OCC019000 BODY, MIND & SPIRIT / Inspiration & Personal Growth
For all educational levels

Cover photo: Gorm Valentin
Author photo: Luca Henskens
Instruments photo, book and cover design: Margriet Naber

The first time I met John Tchicai was in 1989, at a workshop he taught in Rotterdam, where I had studied at the Conservatory. I went to three of his workshops before moving in with him.

At the first workshop I fell in love with his music. It was alive, colorful and strong. There was so much variety in styles, in rhythms and in the ways it was structured. How did he manage to create like that? And how did he manage to do it all in such a relaxed way? I wanted to know more, so the year after I went to a second workshop in Holbæk, a small town in Denmark.

At that second one, I fell in love with John. We danced together during a midweek party and it was so much fun. We invented thousands of steps, and every second was playful. He had nice hands and a strong body; he was great to dance with.

At the third one, another year later, on the west coast of Denmark, we had just become a couple. John asked me if I wanted to go to California with him. He was going to live there for a year and if it worked out, he was hoping to stay longer. I said yes. I hardly knew him, but it felt like a good thing to do.

We moved into an apartment in Davis, a university town in Northern California. We played and composed music and I learned a lot. I had a formal musical education in Rotterdam and was a qualified teacher, but the things I learned when I started living and playing with John were very different from what I'd learned before. They were very practical and very hands-on. I started writing a journal about it so that I wouldn't forget. John was happy when he saw that. He said: "Later on, you can use these notes to write a book and you can call it *Music of Love and Improvisation.*"

Little by little, I got to know John better and found out more about his rich past, full of interesting things. One time, while he was talking to friends about certain events in his life that were so unusual and unique, I said: "John, there should be a book written about you." He smiled but said: "Oh, I'm not old enough for that yet. I'm not done living yet." I suggested I should write that book, and he just laughed. But from that moment on, I paid extra attention to everything that had happened to him, where he played, when and with whom, everything he told me about his earlier life. Somewhere in my mind, I kept track of everything I found out, so that just in case someone ever came to me and asked for information for a book, I'd be ready. Nobody has asked me this question yet, and nobody wrote a book about John either, so now I'm writing it myself.

I'm John's fourth ex-wife. I lived and worked together with him for many years. I remember a concert we did in France with two young Danish musicians, when the local TV station wanted to broadcast an item about John. Two journalists spoke with him and then asked to interview the other musicians, too. I got up and told them I was ready. "Oh, not you," they said. "You're his wife. You're biased. You're only going to say how great he is." When I told them I'd worked with John for a much longer time than those two young Danish men and that I knew John as a person in his daily life quite well, they changed their minds. At least I could speak French and they wouldn't have to translate my speech. In the end they opened their segment with me talking about John's daily life.

There are two main reasons why I believe it's important to make this book available. First, because John's work can still make people happy; second, because people can still learn from it. Musicians looking to find their individual way of making music can learn from John's way of composing and improvising. Everybody else may learn from it as well, because, don't we all compose our own lives? Sometimes it can be necessary to use improvisation for dealing with unforeseen circumstances. Wouldn't it be good if we were more skilled at it? That's why I wrote this book. It's inevitable that my own feelings of love and admiration, or pain (we divorced for a reason), shine through the text. I just hope it won't disturb the message.

John was very active and productive all through his life. In a career of over 50 years he recorded more than 150 albums and performed with many musicians for many different audiences in many different settings all over the world. He was a unique man, a pioneer who lived a happy life with as much freedom as possible.

This book is based on my personal experiences with John and on what he told me, on memories and on notes about my life with him. It's also based on conversations and correspondence with his friends, colleagues and family; on books and documentaries; and on the enormous amount of material he left when he died, including manuscripts, recordings, documents, magazines, his own notes and his appointment diaries from every year since 1968.

I hope this book will inspire readers to allow more loving freedom and improvisation into their own music and lives.

MARGRIET NABER

Introduction - A chaos with some kind of order

The doctor asked: "What is your relationship to the patient?"

"I'm his ex-wife," I told her.

"Oh. Will there be any other women coming here today?"

"I don't think so."

"Okay. Well..."

A few hours later, I had to go out to see my son, our son. When I came back, the nurses gave me a chair in which I could lie down and get some rest while John lay breathing calmly. I heard noises from all the machines in John's room and in the rooms nearby. The combination made a mixture of noises like a *beep-beep-beep, chuuuud, deeedop, deee-dop, chuueed, deeedop, beep* while nurses were walking back and forth. It dawned on me that for the first time in a long time, I was going to spend the night with John, and I fell asleep.

A nurse came in and said he was turning off one of the three monitoring machines "so that the noise wouldn't disturb us", because its meter had gone down to zero and it had begun to beep. I said, "Uh-uh," and dozed off again. Soon he was back, with a more urgent message: *"Madame, votre mari est en train de mourir!* (Your husband is dying!)" Right away, but still a little sleepy, I sat up. I held John's shoulder and caressed his arm. His breathing was very calm and much slower than before I'd fallen asleep. The blood pressure machine indicated zero, and the heartbeat curve had become an almost straight line. John looked fine and very peaceful. Then for one second, he held his breath, it was almost as if he was going to say something. But he followed it with a "swoosh" of air. That was his last out-breath.

I noticed myself thinking: "That wasn't scary at all!"

The next day was bright and sunny. I saw the mountains and it felt like John was sitting right on top of one of them, looking over the valley, smiling happily. Free from a painful body that had kept him in bed for months. Free to go wherever the spirit wanted.

As if he'd made one giant leap from the hospital bed right to the top of the mountain.

John Tchicai, a 76-year-old musician, had been on his way to the airport in Barcelona when he had a stroke and landed in the hospital. At first, he recovered well because he could talk and could move the right side of his body. After a week, by ambulance, he was moved to the hospital in Perpignan, close to where he lived. When we first visited him there, he was upbeat and said: "The ambulance trip sounded like a recording session! Machines and wires... all the noises! Now, did you eat already? Let's go get a bite to eat. There's got to be some sort of cantina here. "

"Maybe you're not good enough for that yet," I said hesitantly. The doctor had just told me John wasn't allowed to eat or drink."

"Oh? I think I'm okay now." John was surprised.

But then he began to sleep a lot more. He got complications, fevers and infections. Some days he was doing very well, but the day after he'd get a fever and be ten steps back again. He couldn't swallow anymore, couldn't eat real food or drink a glass of water, and he was fed through tubes. After two months, he went to a convalescent clinic for revalidation. There he really woke up. He talked with the people around him and he actively tried to re-learn moving his body. We could spend quality time together. But he still couldn't swallow and the artificial food wasn't enough for a man of his height (1m94).

Three months after his stroke, with more complications, he was taken back to the hospital's geriatric department and he became unconscious. The doctors decided to perform surgery. They put him into an artificial coma, connected him to a breathing machine, and prepared him for an operation the next day.

Up until the stroke, John had been a very active man. He was still working as a musician and touring a lot, and all his life he'd been full of initiative. John was strong. Apart from the stroke, he was in relatively good health. He was loved by many, and he had children.

Part of me didn't want him to recover from the operation. Even if it was successful, the convalescence would be long and the recovery perhaps only partial, and John would be dependent on others for the rest of his life. He might not like that.

The next day, I went for a walk in the fields nearby. It was a beautiful day. The sun was shining, the sky was clear and the landscape -- with its river, trees and vineyards – looked harmonious. There was a village nearby and there were mountains in the distance. The atmosphere reminded me of one of John's pieces, called "A Chaos with Some Kind of Order". It's a very relaxed and peaceful composition and it has words to it. In the text, John expresses his love for life and nature, and his dreams for the world. The music is very open and free.

This composition captures the essence of who John was. He wrote, played and recorded it a good 15 years earlier. Other people in the world had performed it.

I thought of the people who knew John: his family and friends, his fellow musicians, his fans out in the world. A lot of them probably didn't even know he was ill. If John died, it would come as a shock to them. Back home, I looked the score up and emailed it to about 30 people all around the world. I asked them, musicians and non-musicians alike, to play, sing or chant it for John, thereby creating a flow of positive energy for him, and for ourselves, too. They responded. One friend in California recited it out in the woods at a spot John liked. A friend in Denmark recited it at home by the light of a candle lit for John. One musician had played it at a concert the previous night. A group of friends in California recorded it for John and sent me the mp3, which I downloaded and played for John at the hospital.

After the operation, John didn't speak or move any more. But he could open his eyes and he could listen to the musical vibrations from friends around the world.

A group in Seattle recorded it the day John was dying. We played that recording at the funeral.

One of the reasons I like this composition so much is that I've seen it grow. Combining text and music, from a short melody it became a piece for a large group. With its important role for improvisation, it sounded different every time it was played.

The melody was born one sunny morning in the spring of 1994 when we lived in Davis. John and I were playing our instruments. He was playing bamboo flute and I had my keyboard. He asked me to use an airy sound and play a drone (a long sustained tone). He asked me to play in Db because this not very common key was the tuning of his bamboo flute. So, I held a low Db pressed in while we improvised, and little by little, John created some melodic phrases that he kept coming back to.

When we stopped, John said: "That was nice. This is going somewhere. We should keep this for a composition. Margriet, can you write these melodies down, with your beautiful handwriting?" I could and I did. On the score, you can see my handwriting of John's notes.

We played it with the group we had at that time, called John Tchicai and the Archetypes. It was a seven-piece with two electric guitars, electric bass, percussion, drums, saxophone and keyboard. John and I played the melody, and the other instruments played rhythms, chords, other sounds and improvisations. In the first part there was no steady beat, just a sound field in which the melodic fragments floated around. Then bass and drums set up a rhythmic groove and we played the melody line in the middle, and there were solos. After that, the rhythm slowed down, the field opened up again and we played the last melody line, until the piece came to a rest with a fade-out. We performed it in public a few times. The groove was different every time and the improvisations were different, of course, so it had a lot of feel for the moment.

The text on the score is John's handwriting. He added it later, notating it in the way he developed when teaching kids in an elementary school near Davis. He wanted them to recite text in a rhythmical way and in unison, everybody at the same time. He could have written it in standard musical notation, but the kids didn't read that, so John developed this way of writing text in a grid of boxes. Every box corresponds to a beat, so that one row of four boxes together is a 4/4 measure. The exact place where the word is written -- for instance at the beginning, in the middle or just in front of the next box -- tells you when to recite it, in relation to the beat.

For "A Chaos with Some Kind of Order", John wrote the poem in the same box structure so it could be recited rhythmically together with the rest of the music, by non-musician readers. It was a hit with the large workshop group he began teaching around that time. There were about 20 people in the group, including a few singers, and it worked out very well.

In 1998, the composition was beautifully recorded in Denmark by John with Ok Nok Kongo, a group of five wind instruments, guitar, bass and drums. It came out on the album *Moonstone Journey*. John also performed it with other groups, and sometimes had the audience recite the poem with him, translated in other languages if needed. After John's death, I performed it with students and other printmakers near my home in France.

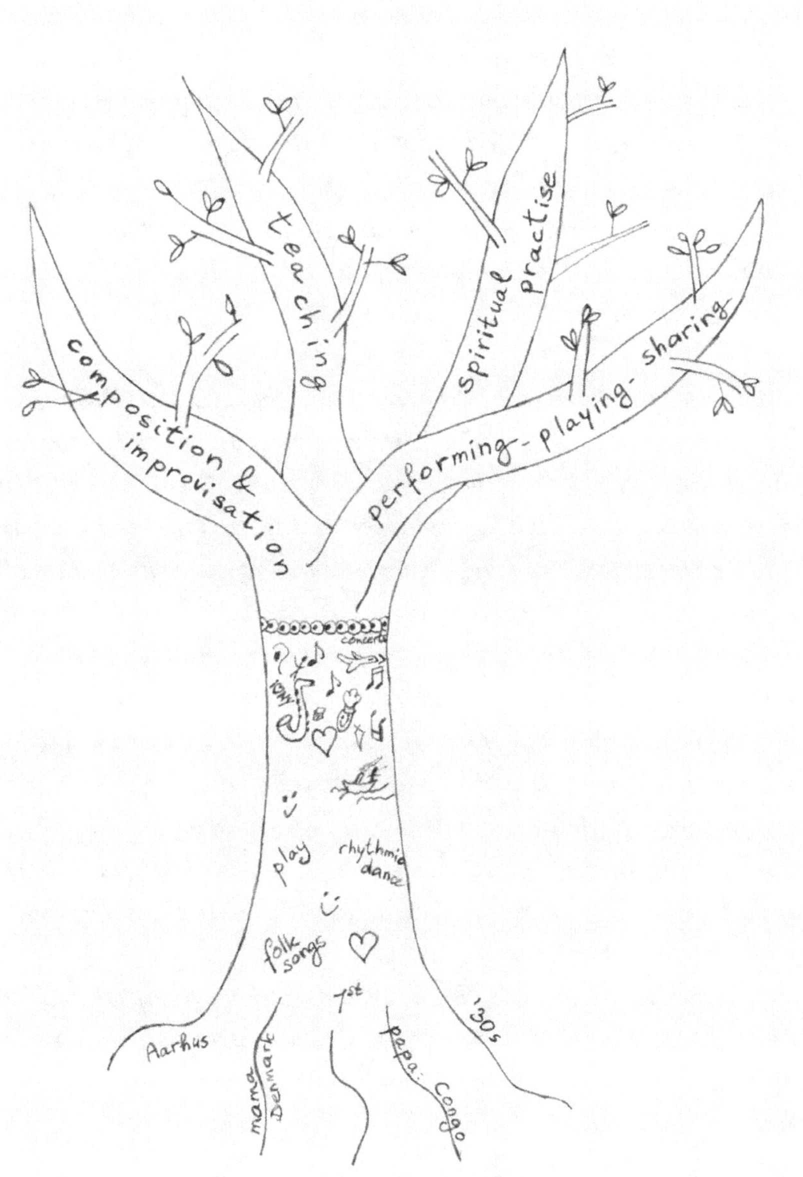

composition & improvisation
teaching
spiritual practise
performing - playing - sharing
concert
play
rhythmic dance
folk songs
1st
'30s
Aarhus
mama Denmark
pepa Congo

I like to compare John's life to a tree.

John loved nature very much. We often went on trips into nature, to a forest, a river or the sea, taking coffee and cakes and a book or writing material along. John drove. He was a good driver and very good at finding just that particular side road which led to a nice place, a view or a hiking path. He'd take that side road, drive to the end of it, then park the car and we'd be at a beautiful spot to relax.

I've been trying to cultivate that capacity, too. During one of my walks, one early evening last winter, I saw silhouettes of trees, and it struck me I saw John there. A firmly rooted tree, with a trunk, main branches, side branches and many smaller and smaller branches. A tree that has leaves, flowers and seeds that come and go with the seasons. It is strong and stable and able to survive in different weather types.

The roots were formed by his parents and the culture in Denmark in the 1940s. John's parents were of different races and nationalities, and John's tree didn't look the same as most other trees in Denmark. With the nourishment of love, family, friends and music, he grew up nicely, and when he was sixteen, he bought a saxophone. Playing music became his passion.

Eventually, after John decided to make it his profession, he felt that he needed to play with some of the more adventurous American jazz musicians. So he moved to New York, and jumped right into the cooking and melting pot. He was very active. In collaboration with other musicians he created a way of free improvisation that had not been heard before. He recorded nine albums in three years, several of them historically important. In these years in New York he developed his musical philosophy.

When he returned from New York, the trunk was complete and John branched out. He found new musicians to play with in Denmark and other countries. In concerts and recordings he communicated his music to audiences world-wide.

Sometimes John picked up his instrument and just improvised freely. But he also liked to structure the music, so he began composing. In his hundreds of compositions, there was always space for improvisation, for fresh input from the moment.

It was very clear to him that music and life had a deep meaning. He turned to Eastern philosophy and started yoga and meditation which became integral parts of his life and his music. Often he used spiritual texts in his compositions.

People were drawn to him and his new, innovative way of playing, and they wanted to learn from him. He became a music teacher at elementary schools, universities and prisons. He led workshops and student orchestras all over the world.

These activities became the main branches of the John tree. All acquired side branches, flowers, leaves and seeds. John left an impression on many of the people he came in contact with, and now those impressions are being taken forward. Fans still play his recordings, his students use the seeds of knowledge they gained from him, musicians still play his compositions. The tree lives on.

1

PLAYING HIS WAY TO NEW YORK

John made his first footprints in Denmark. He was born in its capital, Copenhagen, in 1936. His mother, Ketty Jensen, was Danish, and his father, Joseph Tchicai, was Congolese. On John's second birthday his little brother Mauritz was born and soon after that they moved to Aarhus, a harbour town on the Jutland peninsula.

When John and I got together, he was very generous with compliments about my looks so I asked: "Do you know how cute you look yourself?" He, 54 years old, was silent for a while and then he told me he won the first prize in a photo contest when he was two.

It was a playful answer, but it was true. When John was growing up, there were few people of mixed race in Denmark and most children were blond with blue eyes. One day a local photographer organized a photo contest for children, where the winner could have free photo sessions, once a year for seven years. Ketty decided to take John in to have

John, 1938

his photo taken, and that photo won the prize. That's why there are professionally taken portraits of him and Mauritz as young boys growing up.

The Tchicais lived in a small apartment in a four-story building on what were then the outskirts of Aarhus. There were many families in the building, and lots of kids for John and Mauritz to play with. When they were small, they played in the sandbox in the courtyard. Then they rode their bikes around it, and still later they crossed the street, because on the other side there was a building site, a carpenter's shop and lots of nature. It was a paradise for kids.

The Tchicai family, 1940

John told me once, when talking about his concept of music, that you always need to have some rules. The rules can be loose or very detailed, but there have to be rules. He said: "Without rules, there is no game. That counts for music just as it counts for children who're playing." And he invented all kinds of games and rules.

Preben Brandsborg, who as a kid lived next door to the Tchicai family, remembers: "Both John and Mauritz were very inventive. When my father came home, he would stick his head out of the window, because he enjoyed looking at these two boys playing.

John and brother Mauritz, ±1942

We played in the bushes and imagined we were in the African jungle. Later, we had a hiding place in the basement of the building, under the staircase, and decided it was a submarine. We believed we were sitting on the bottom of the sea. No doubt, John was the leader of the group.

Once he suggested making an underground cave on the construction zone from where we could contemplate future plans. We dug it and it had several tunnels. We were going to spend the night there but our parents found out and the cave was destroyed. Good thinking, because that night there was a thunderstorm. Then we built a small village consisting of grass huts on the field. We played Cowboys and Indians with bows and arrows, with the kids of an adjacent building, and often we won. John, who was already tall, protected the kids who were a little younger."

One day, when John was nine, Mauritz wanted to find out what matches tasted like. He ate the sulphur, got severe blood poisoning and was taken to the hospital. In the state hospital he didn't get better so his worrying parents had him transfered to another hospital run by Catholic nuns. When Mauritz recovered after two months, their father was so grateful that he transferred the boys to a Catholic school and both of them had to become altar boys in church. This led to another game John played with his friends.

"John said we should be baptized in the river," Preben said. "Before we left home, everybody made a wooden spear and a shield. With painted faces, we went down to the river in a long row, John at the front, Mauritz at the back, and the white boys in the middle. All the way down, we sort of moved our spear up and down and flashed the shield and then came the war cry: 'Umba, umba, kilde mig i rumba, Umba, umba, kilde mig i rumba.' It went on like this and people were looking at us -- they saw us from their bicycles and cars and thought, 'They must be crazy.' But we had a great time. At the river, we were pushed into the water and everybody was baptized. I was called Prebsu. Rats were swimming around us in the water, but we didn't pay attention to it. The only one who was not in the river was John. He stood on the side, just laughing. That was ok, why not?"

The boys were already musically active. "We played music on a comb with special paper around it. We played the blues and John was our music teacher. He had a radio, and we searched for short-wave stations on it. There you could hear unusual music. Thinking back now, I think it was klezmer, or gypsy-music, Oriental or Greek, but at that time, we didn't know what kind of music it was. So John and Mauritz decided to call it 'Negro music'."

They had a lot of fun, but sometimes people complained about them and called the police, saying "those black boys did it", and then the police would come to their house to talk with Ketty and Joseph.

When they were a little bigger, they went out on their bikes towards a lake, a few kilometers outside of Aarhus. In summer they swam there, caught clam shells and freshwater shrimp, and rowed boats. In winter, they skated on the ice. As teenagers they roller-skated in a rink, and John once won a prize for that, too. They never did any team sports like soccer. They didn't like that.

Ketty Jensen,
John's mother

Ketty worked at home and took care of the family and the house. Sometimes she did ironing for other families in the building. She had a beautiful smile. "Ketty was a very lovable woman," Preben said. "She was always busy and she walked fast everywhere. But whenever I passed, she greeted me: 'Hello, Preben, how do you do today?' She was always smiling."

Ketty loved to sing and she had a nice voice. She often sang Danish folk songs around the house and John liked listening to her. These very melodious songs became a foundation stone of his musical development.

She had been born in Hillerød, a town surrounded by forests filled with birds, not far from Copenhagen and close to the sea. In summer, she took the boys there to spend the vacation with their grandparents. They were instilled with a spiritual awareness and with respect for religion and nature and a sense of humility towards the world around them.

The boys' father stayed in Aarhus to work. Joseph was a doorman and a restroom attendant at a restaurant. He had never gone to school because he was born in the Congolese jungle, probably in or around 1885, near a town called Tchicai in the Loango region. The people were called Tchicaya.

He had left his home because his father was a chief, and according to a local custom, when he died his eldest son would have to kill all the younger sons before becoming king. Joseph had a talent for languages and became a translator for the German ethnographer Leo Frobenius, who travelled up and down the Congo river. When Frobenius asked him to come to Europe and work for him, Joseph said yes.

They went to Germany together, but once they were there, Joseph was treated more or less like a slave, so he left. He went to

Joseph Tchicai, John's father with John

Denmark, learned the language and met a nice Danish woman. However, when she got pregnant, her parents wouldn't allow her to marry a black man. That was in 1913. John's eldest half-brother Kaj Timmermann was born, but grew up with little contact with his father. Joseph met another woman and they married. They had seven children together but eventually they divorced.

Then one day in 1934 or 1935, Joseph met Ketty in a park near Copenhagen, where she was having coffee with a friend on a terrace. Suddenly Joseph kneeled down next to her and said in his low voice: "I love you." Before long they were married.

Joseph didn't sing, nor did he speak any African languages -- he knew several -- to the children, but he had a knack for percussion. He was known for playing music on the doors of the restaurant where he worked. Film critic/musician Niels Holt remembers: "Upstairs was the restaurant with the tables and chairs, where musicians were playing. Downstairs were the toilets were John's father worked. He played drum rhythms on the doors, using the different parts of his two hands to create different sounds: his fingers, the ball of his thumb, the palm of his hands. And one of the toilet doors had a very good sound, better than the others. When that toilet was free, John's father played intricate rhythms on its door. People, including myself, came downstairs just to listen to him. He was known for it. He did it for fun."

Mauritz doesn't remember his father playing percussion at home, but he recalls: "When our father was happy, he stood up, grabbed a chair, held it in front of him and danced with it. He danced in a rhythmical, bouncing way. He never danced in European partner style with my mother."

I can recognize that way of dancing in the way John danced. And African rhythms became another foundation stone of John's musical development.

Kaj Timmermann, John's much older half-brother, also had a feeling for rhythm. He became a drummer and played in a swing band in the late '30s and '40s. This group, called the Harlem Kiddies, was famous in Denmark. It was a mixed band with two other black players, which was not common in Denmark then (actually they were also mulatto, like Kaj). They were popular during the war, when Denmark was under German occupation.

When John was about eight, and the Harlem Kiddies were playing in Aarhus, Joseph took his family to see Kaj's band. John was very impressed, and very proud to have a big brother who could play the drums like that. Later he noted: "It must've been one of the few Danish bands that could swing in an African-American way." Kaj was also the manager of the group, but by the late '40s he gave it up, saying it was too hard to find bookings. He became a barman instead and also worked as

School photograph, ±1947

a solo piano player in bars and clubs. Later, when John had started playing the saxophone, he and Kaj jammed a few times.

When John was ten, one day Joseph came home with a violin and
told John and Mauritz he had signed them up for violin lessons. The
boys went, but it didn't interest them very much. When they had to
practise at home, they did it in the basement and took turns: while one
brother played the violin, the other one read comic books. Soon they
gave up the violin.

During the war Denmark was occupied by Germany, and German
soldiers were stationed in Aarhus. John said about this: "Concerning
what it could've been like to be black during the war, first of all, although our father was so-called black, I and my brothers and sisters
were not black but brown. My father was very popular and known by
a lot of people in both Copenhagen and Aarhus—in part because at
the time there were few negroes in Denmark. He made many German

friends during the war, partly because they frequented the restaurants he worked at and partly because he spoke German. I even seem to remember German soldiers visiting our home. My brother Mauritz and I used to play near the freight train station in Aarhus, which the Germans were in charge of. Sometimes the guards asked us to go to the bakery for them and they tipped us for it."

The boys' father also took them to the harbour, where big ships came in from all over the world. When American ships arrived, the black crew members often invited Joseph and his sons on board. They played jazz records and had interesting food and they gave the children chewing gum and other nice things. Joseph spoke with them in English.

Joseph worked in the evenings and came home in the middle of the night. During the day, he had to sleep. This meant the boys had to be quiet. When a neighbour played Chopin nocturnes on his piano at that hour, Joseph took a hammer that was lying next to the couch for this purpose, and gave a few bangs on the heating pipes. That made him stop. Joseph had a strong voice. The boys went to the cinema now and then, and if Joseph went with them to a funny movie, and started laughing, the boys were embarrassed because his laugh was very loud and everyone would turn to look at them.

Making sounds in the movie house was common though at that time, and it seems John already had a social conscience. "Every Sunday afternoon we went to the cinema," Preben said. "We saw Laurel and Hardy, that was a good laugh, but we went to lots of cowboy and Indian films, too. And we decided, meeting in our headquarters submarine, to back up the Indians, because we boys, we sat in the first three rows. And when the cowboys came on screen, most of the boys shouted and cheered the cowboys. But when the Indians did well, we cheered."

Sometimes people stared at John and Mauritz in the streets. They were curious about their color. People sometimes asked Ketty and Joseph if they could touch the boys' hair, but the parents didn't like that. Sometimes people pointed at them in the street, saying 'Look, there are some negroes!' That made Joseph mad and, in his low, loud voice and broken Danish, he told them to stop staring. Then they stopped.

If John and Mauritz did something that made Joseph mad, he beat them with his belt. When the boys saw it coming, they ran behind the dinner table. Joseph ran after them while Ketty stood in the way, trying to stop Joseph and spare the children. But Joseph's strong will was the law of the house.

As John grew up, it turned out he had strong opinions and a strong will, too. He started arguing with his father. His father said: "That boy will make a big accident one day!" When John was 16, and his regular school years were over, he wanted to become a cook on an ocean-going ship. But Joseph said: "You're going to a cook's school. I found you an apprenticeship at a restaurant in town and you're starting this Monday." On that occasion, John had to accept his father's decision. But another time, when the argument had gone too far, John ran off. He went to one of the ferry boats that sailed between Aarhus and Denmark's main island, Sjælland. He asked if he could work on it, and he stayed away from home for three months. His parents accepted his choice and let him do it. After three months he came back, and then things became more peaceful.

It was in this time that John discovered jazz and discovered the saxophone. He was 14 when Niels Holt first crossed paths with him. "I saw John walk in the streets of Aarhus. He worked as a delivery boy for a shop and was pushing a hand cart with merchandise on it. Abruptly, I asked him: 'Do you know jazz?' John looked at me, then turned away after this odd question. But the next time we met, we got talking. By then I was 19, a music-theory student at the Conservatory of Aarhus, and I told John about an event there every Wednesday evening, when people played jazz. One evening John showed up, standing in the doorway, long and thin. He was shy. I asked him to come in. He did, and he started coming to this event regularly."

John told me his first inspiration to play jazz came from hearing Billie Holiday sing "Strange Fruit". He also said he was drawn to the sound of the saxophone because he liked, as he put it, "the type of creativity you could hear from saxophone players."

Thanks to the role played by improvisation, jazz compositions never sound the same way twice. Often, there's a written theme followed by improvisations on that theme, usually by one player after another. Those are called solos. Then the theme is played again and that's the end of the piece. What you play in the solo is based on the theme and on the chords that harmonize it, but other than that, the soloists can do what they want, what they feel like playing on that particular day.

John bought an alto saxophone and started to practise. He went back to the basement where he and Mauritz used to practise the violin, this time without comic books but absorbed in the saxophone. He listened to the radio a lot and started buying jazz LPs. He also started going to concerts and sometimes those concerts were in Copenhagen, the capital, which lies on Sjælland. But if you wanted to go there, you always had to cross the water from Aarhus. Maybe when John ran off to get a job on the ferry, it had to do with wanting to go to those concerts. When he lived on board the ferry, it was easier to hop off on the Sjælland side and go to Copenhagen.

In 1953, he saw some famous jazz orchestras in Copenhagen, like the big band of Lionel Hampton and the Stan Kenton Orchestra, which featured the alto saxophonist Lee Konitz. John became a great fan of Konitz, and of his work with the pianist Lennie Tristano and the tenor saxophonist Warne Marsh. Much later, he would take lessons with him.

That year, Joseph had a stroke. He recovered from it, but a second stroke in 1954 was fatal. After his passing, John, Mauritz and their mother kept living in the apartment. When I asked John how it was when his father died, he said to me: "I remember I bought a bucket of red paint, and painted the walls of my room red."

His friend of those days, the pianist Jørn-Erik Jensen, remembers this: "We met in a music shop in Aarhus. It was impossible to miss each other because the shop was the size of a big closet. John was a Charlie Parker fan at that time. We were young and used to walk up and down the streets enjoying the cozy shops. There were not many cars at that time, but there were very nice girls. We would go to John's house, we would have tea with some bread and jam, and listen to his Charlie Parker albums, or to his other favorite album called *Wow*, with Lennie Tristano, Lee Konitz and [the guitarist] Billy Bauer. John had painted his room very dramatically with big, red motifs, very impressive. We used to whistle and sing different musical ideas as we walked around town.

"I remember hearing John play bebop with his brother Kaj Timmermann's group the Harlem Kiddies, just once, not regularly. John liked to hear me play classical music. I remember a very sunny day, the piano was standing by the window, and I played Sinding's *Frühlingsrauschen* and Chopin's Opus 66, *Fantaisie Impromptu*. Another time, an evening when the piano was standing up the wall, he asked me to play like Fats Waller, Erroll Garner and a couple of others. He thought it was funny.

But when he was serious, he liked me to play in a Tristano way. John was very open and always smiling. As a friend, there was no better."

By 1955, after training as a cook for four years and obtaining his diploma, John had decided to try and make a career as a jazz musician and he applied to the Conservatory in Aarhus. At the time, the conservatories only taught classical music, and saxophones weren't admitted. But clarinets were, so John played the clarinet, which has similar fingering, and learned music history, music theory and some piano. He passed the first year, but quit during the second year when he had to practise a Von Weber composition that he really disliked. He decided to go his own way, finding a job

Graduating as a chef-cook, 1955

as a cook and using his free time to play, listen to and practise as much of the music he loved as he could. At that time the most fashionable jazz style was bebop, and John, like many other young jazz musicians, tried to play in the highly complex, very technical style of Charlie Parker.

One night he was playing in a bar when a young woman named Annette Sidenius was sitting in the audience. She was 18 and had come to Aarhus to train as a nurse. "A friend of mine said I should come along to this bar where they had jazz concerts, because a very good group with a special saxophonist would be playing. So, I came along, even though jazz didn't interest me. When I saw John I thought he was the most handsome guy in the world."

She tried to get his attention and succeeded. Soon they became a couple, but there was a problem. The nurses' school was run by nuns, and male visitors were not allowed. Nor were students allowed to spend the night outside the school. Annette could only continue her studies and live with John if they got married, which they decided to do. But in 1957, women in Denmark still had to get permission from their parents if they wanted to marry. When they went to Annette's parents to ask permission for her to marry John, they were met with a refusal. Annette said: "If you don't give me your permission to marry John, I'm going to live with him anyway." She moved in with John, Mauritz and Ketty. She had to leave the nurse school and found a job as a secretary.

In 1958 John was called up to do his military service and he chose to do it in the navy. He could choose in which part of Denmark he wanted to be, and he nominated Sjælland in order to be closer to the jazz scene of Copenhagen.

The navy granted his choice, and since they knew he was a musician, they gave him a job as a musician in the navy band, a privileged job with more free time and better food. John played the big bass drum in the marching band at rehearsals and performances, and he didn't have to do the regular sailors' work. He had time to go to Copenhagen and listen to music.

But he was stationed in the very north of the island, and going to Copenhagen wasn't easy. There were buses and trains he could take, but they stopped running later in the evening, so it was practically impossible to go to a concert and be back at the base in time. John went anyway, got back too late and was punished for it, locked up in solitary confinement for a few days or a week. He once told me that this was the only period in his life where he was seriously depressed.

Denmark is a kingdom and the king at that time, Frederik IX, was known for being an arts lover. He was a good pianist and sometimes he conducted orchestras. He was also known for being accessible: on Sundays he would ride a horse in the parks of Copenhagen, and if you wanted to talk with him, you could stop him for a conversation.

Annette decided to write him a letter. She asked the king if John could be stationed in Copenhagen instead of in the North, so he could be close to the capital's jazz scene. The king granted her wish and John was relocated to Copenhagen. He lost his preferential musician's job and had to do kitchen work instead, making meatballs for the other sailors. But he got permission to go out and play his own music in town, as long as he wore his naval uniform.

He still had to deal with schedules, because the naval base was on Holmen, an island of Copenhagen, and he needed to take a ferry to get there from the town centre. Sometimes he missed it, but he was happy again. He went to concerts and rehearsed with Copenhagen-based musicians. One of the places where they rehearsed was called Danmarks Musikskole, on Copenhagen's pedestrian street near Kongens Nytorv. It was there that Pierre Dørge, then a 13-year-old guitar student, saw him for the first time.

"One day someone said we should go up to the fourth floor," Pierre says, "because a jazz group was rehearsing there, and -- like people said at that time -- there was a 'real negro' playing. We went up, and there was a giant man in a white navy-uniform playing the alto saxophone. They played Parker songs, like 'Ornithology', and 'Night in Tunisia'. You could see John was a person with charisma. And the guitar player was playing a real Gibson guitar, which was impossible to pay for in those days. The next Sunday afternoon, they were going to play in a jam session at a jazz club called Vingaarden. I went there and asked my other musician friends to come along. It was fantastic to hear John play, but I was too shy to ask him anything."

After his time in the navy was over, John moved in with Annette in a small apartment in Copenhagen. He found a day job as a cook, and the rest of the time he worked on music as much as possible. He took lessons at the music school with Ib Glindemann, a leading Danish jazz musician at the time.

Home-transcription of jazz-standard "Stablemates"

To handle bebop, a musician needed to be able to play fast and follow rapid chord changes. It was the standard approach, but there were others who played in a different way, like Lennie Tristano and Lee Konitz, and John had been listening to them. There was also Ornette Coleman, who took the principles of modern jazz in a different direction. He retained the powerful and sophisticated rhythmic flow but moved away from regular harmonic structures and chord sequences. His priority was to have a sense of natural melodic invention in the music.

John continued going to the Sunday jam sessions at Vingaarden. Saxophonist Karsten Vogel saw him there: "I remember clearly, they played Tadd Dameron's 'Hot House', based on 'What Is This Thing Called Love?', which was one of the bebop anthems. If you played bebop, you should also play 'Hot House'. And they played that, and that was the first time I heard him play. I was impressed by the sound and also that he really played this bebop. He played it in such a convincing way, I was really impressed. Wow! He can play the alto saxophone. He was not copying Charlie Parker. One of the first things I thought was, this guy's got a really good sound in his saxophone.

"When John quickly became well known in Copenhagen as this good saxophone player that he was, he met Max Brüel, who played tenor sax at that time. Max Brüel was the oldest and John was five or six years older than, for example, me. John and Max were the kings of the jam session. When they went on stage... Max Brüel was a very good and very powerful player. And together, these two, they took the scene. They ruled Vingaarden and we could get out there and play two or three songs, that was the kind of jam session, you go play two or three songs, but it was like, in the end of the jam session, for the last half hour, it was John and Max, and that was it, the kings on stage.

"It was a rough competition between musicians on that stage. As it always has been in jazz: cutting contests have been well known in jazz since the '20s, for a hundred years nearly, or more than that. That was the scene. Of course we talked nicely to each other, it's nothing bad, but it was for sure, who's the best? And when Max and John entered the stage, wow, they were the kings of Vingaarden Sunday. They were good! It is important to say that they were good, and it was powerful music."

John played with different musicians, trying to find people who had the same ideas about playing jazz as he had, not necessarily bebop. He recalled "trying to sort of expand the forms of traditional jazz, of bebop jazz, which is where we started. We didn't quite master it, as there were so many chord shifts that were difficult to learn, and which limited us in a way. I had some ideas about a music that was more open and where you had fewer chords, and the melodious material was more at the front, and more a determinant for the development of a sequence."

Musicians like Karsten Vogel and Pierre Dørge liked what John was doing, as did journalists Erik Wiedemann and Torben Ulrich. But not everybody liked it. According to Wiedemann, "John was the most controversial musician in Danish jazz before leaving for New York in late '62." In 2004, John said this: "I was at that time, and probably still am considered an outsider. My style of playing was different from the Danish musicians, and I think they felt my playing was not educated enough and that I started to express myself too early."

Many international musicians were passing through Copenhagen, like Ornette Coleman, Count Basie, Louis Armstrong, Miles Davis, John Coltrane and Eric Dolphy. Several of them settled down in Denmark, including the saxophonists Ben Webster and Dexter Gordon, who lived there for several years. John listened to them. He even hitchhiked to Paris to see Thelonious Monk. When possible, he talked with American musicians.

"Being brown in Denmark made it easier for me to feel at ease with black musicians—something which didn't always come natural to white musicians," John said. "As a young man in Denmark I was also drawn to black people and thought they were funnier, happier, friendlier, more relaxed and strange. It therefore came natural to me to begin socializing with visiting black musicians in Copenhagen during the late 50s and early 60s."

With Max Brüel he started a quintet and named it Jørgen Leth quintet, after a friend and jazz journalist. They played standards that were not typically bebop, like "Night in Tunisia", whose theme features rhythmic repetition. In the spring of 1962, the group was invited to perform at a jazz festival in Warsaw, Poland. Two tracks of this performance ("Blue Monk" and "Night in Tunisia") were released on an EP. This was John's first record, and Pierre Dørge bought it. "Their sound of alto sax and baritone sax together was very nice," he felt. "I could hear John had an unusual sound, a very singing and lyrical sound."

The group was asked to play in Finland that summer, at the International Youth Festival of Helsinki, where they were given a warm reception and won a gold medal. It was there, too, that John met two American musicians, the trumpeter Bill Dixon and the saxophonist Archie Shepp. "Groups from all over the world came and played," he remembered. "And I found out there was an American group playing there, and that turned out to be Bill Dixon with his quartet, with Archie Shepp on tenor and Perry Robinson on clarinet, and Don Moore on bass." John heard them play several times and was very impressed. He later said that when hearing them play, "I saw a power and a sense of rhythm that I never heard from musicians in Europe."

He talked to Dixon and Shepp, who told him that if this was the kind of music he wanted to play, why didn't he come to the States? Then they could play together and he could meet other American musicians. That started something off. In Annette's recollection, "John was playing, thinking and talking about music all the time, and after the trip to Helsinki there was no stopping him. He kept saying: 'I want to go to New York. I need to go to New York to play with people there. Let's move there.'"

It was Annette, a stenographer at the Foreign Ministry, who found a way to get there. Secretaries were sometimes sent out to Danish consulates around the world on three-year contracts, with apartment and moving expenses paid. She decided to apply for such a position at the Danish consulate in New York. That was a much-coveted place, but she succeeded. In October 1962, three days after the Bay of Pigs invasion in Cuba, she arrived in New York. ("There was a strange tension in the air, as a result of the invasion..."). John needed a work visa, so he couldn't join her right away. As soon as she arrived, Annette started looking for a job for him and she found a Swedish restaurant ready to hire him as a cook. John just had to wait for the paperwork to pass. At that same time, in November '62, in Copenhagen the pianist Cecil Taylor's group had a month's long stay at the Jazzhus Montmartre, with Sunny Murray on drums, Jimmy Lyons on alto and the tenorist Albert Ayler sitting in a few times. For John, hearing them was a great experience. Sunny and Albert often came and sat in with John and friends at their Sunday-afternoon jam sessions.

In 2010, John recalled the impact of the drummer in particular: "When Sunny Murray came to Copenhagen in 1962 to play for the whole month of November with Cecil Taylor and Jimmy Lyons, he came as a messenger bringing the good news of how to play drums in a modern way. Finally a drummer with enough sensibility in his mind to be able to play several tempos at the same time, enough energy to stand up to Taylor and Ayler and still keep the feeling of swing, without losing or speeding the tempo up."

2

COOKING IN NEW YORK

On December 14, 1962, John flew to New York for the first time. A city where people from all over the world and all kinds of backgrounds, nationalities and colors were living together was a big contrast to Copenhagen. The tempo of life was faster and there were many more people. It inspired John and he picked up this vibe of speed and action. In three and a half years he played with many jazz musicians, founded two bands, recorded nine LPs, collaborated with other art forms and made two European tours in between.

When John talked about his period in New York, you got the impression it was always sunny and never rained.

John and Annette moved into a one bedroom-apartment on 46th Street and John started work as a cook in the Swedish restaurant in midtown that had vouched for his residency permit. On his second evening in New York, he went to hear soprano saxophonist Steve Lacy, met the trumpeter Don Cherry, and, on the way home, ran into Archie Shepp, whom he had met in Helsinki that summer. Shepp was very friendly and helpful, and told him about other musicians and about occasions and sessions where he could hear and meet people he might like to play with. "I found him very impressive when I first heard him," Shepp said. "John was a very original saxophone player who always had something new to say in his solos." They became friends and started to rehearse together.

In New York, there were many people who, like John, wanted to move beyond the bebop conventions, trying to play jazz in a different way. Jam sessions are a way of meeting and exchanging information, of communicating who you are. John started attend them, listening to how other people were playing. In turn, they heard how he played. In his early weeks in the city he made an impression on several influential members of the scene, including LeRoi Jones, the poet, activist and *Down Beat* columnist, who later changed his name to Amiri Baraka.

Jones/Baraka wrote: "A tall young alto player, John Tchicai, came in out of the cold and blew one of the most startling solos I have ever heard, just to announce his presence. It was apparent, at once, to all within earshot, that we were hearing one of the newest of the new, a musician who had come out of nowhere, with all his music together, as well as his expression."

John sat in for a couple of pieces with a group of trumpeter Don Cherry, drummer Billy Higgins and bassist Wilbur Ware, and "brought the audience to its feet", according to Baraka. "Even though he is a Negro, Tchicai is a Danish citizen. He plays the alto like he wanted to sound like Coleman Hawkins playing like Ornette Coleman. But he sounds mostly like nothing you've heard before. There's no doubt in my mind that a lot of people are going to hear him very soon."

Shepp remembers: "John brought part of his history as a black man with him. I could think of him as a black man, but there were other aspects to his roots that were also European. It made him a very special person." In February of 1963, John joined his and Bill Dixon's ensemble and played for a broadcast at the radio station WBAI. That summer he had four programs on the same station with his own "John Tchicai Quartet" including Archie Shepp, Jimmy Stevenson on bass and Sunny Murray on drums.

John wanted to develop his talents and his musical ideas from all sides. He and Annette lived close to the Museum of Modern Art of New York, and John often went there, just to sit down in front of a painting (for instance a Jackson Pollock) and contemplate. He became close friends with the Surinamese painter Jan Quintus Telting, who was married to a colleague friend of Annette's. Telting was a painter but also a jazz fan, and together they went to concerts and to exhibitions of visual art.

In New York, John began experimenting with making his first compositions. He wrote them down in pencil on manuscript paper so that he could rub out any mistakes with an eraser and he recorded and listened to them using his first tape recorder.

He also spent time listening to records, alone or together with friends. "Other musicians often came to our apartment to hang out," Annette said. "The fact I could easily get alcohol through my work at the consulate might have played a role. But when they were there, they listened to music, they talked about music, and when they left, it was to go play or listen to music somewhere."

At the same time, John kept in touch with people he knew in Denmark. He was a faithful letter-writer. When the managers of the Jazzhus Montmartre heard that he was now playing with Shepp and others, they became interested and said, if he could get a band together with those musicians, they would book them in Copenhagen in the fall.

Shepp remembered that "John came up with the idea to create this group called the New York Contemporary Five, which was composed of J.C. Moses on drums, Don Moore on bass, Don Cherry on trumpet, myself as a tenor saxophone and John on alto."

They practised through the summer. It went well, and all they needed was a place to get live experience by performing to an audience. A gig was hard to find. They played one, at Café Harouts in Greenwich Village, and one at the Danish consulate, where Annette worked.

She and John had married at New York's City Hall in March. Even in New York City, mixed couples were still a rare sight. The US was still segregated and racial differences were a significant factor in daily life. John and Annette weren't used to that. In Denmark they were used to openness, but in New York when they were out in public, sometimes they attracted strange looks.

John remembered how, in the beginning, he was also shocked to discover another aspect of American society as it related to artists, and jazz musicians in particular: "I knew very little about American life. So when I came to the Lower East Side for the first time, and saw how people lived there, I was very surprised, because I had thought that people who can play that wonderfully, they couldn't live, like, in very poor neighborhoods. I thought that they would be living in nice houses and have nice cars and everything."

Annette talked with her boss: "John was trying to find concerts where he could perform his music. At the consulate there were parties regularly, often with live music. I told my boss John played jazz and he had a group. At the occasion of a visit by some European guests, my boss booked them, and so it came about that John's group, with Archie Shepp and Don Cherry, played their music at a party at the Danish consulate. The guests were mostly from Europe. They had a different attitude than people in the US. When John's group played, the musicians

Don Cherry, Archie Shepp and John Tchicai with friends. New York, 1963

were treated with respect and the party afterwards with guests and musicians was fun. The American musicians, who were all black, were not used to socializing with these European upper-class 'important' people who were all white, and they seemed to like the evening a lot. I have a clear memory of us, afterwards, standing in the elevator going down. They looked so happy."

In September the New York Contemporary Five arrived in Copenhagen and played for five weeks at Jazzhus Montmartre, with gigs in smaller towns in Denmark and Sweden in between, and a concert in Stockholm in November. The chance to play together every evening allowed their music to develop much faster. Archie Shepp enjoyed the experience: "The club was full every night, and it was a good time for the music. When we went to the Montmartre, we replaced Dexter Gordon, who had been there for six months. That night club was always fun. I think we had a good feeling on the recording; we were all very young at the time, but I think we gave it our very best."

Two evenings were recorded and a first album was released on the Sonet label in 1964. At Archie's request, they held off from releasing a second volume until later. The reasoning was that once their careers had taken off, they could negotiate a better price. A few years later the Danish filmmaker Niels Holt included one track of these recordings in his film *Futura One*.

On these recordings, John can be heard developing his own approach by improvising on motifs. He would create a motif and then repeat it, while always making variations on it -- for example, by playing the last note on a different pitch or with a different rhythmic stress. He was beginning to use that idea before he went to New York – there are early traces of it in his solo on "Night in Tunisia" on the recording made in Poland with the Jørgen Leth quintet in 1962 -- but now he was letting go of the theme and chord progressions of the song much more than before.

Don Cherry giving a cue during a NYC5 TV-recording in Copenhagen. John Tchicai, J.C. Moses, Don Moore, Don Cherry, Archie Shepp, 1963
©Jan Persson

Saxophonist Charlie Kohlhase described the difference: "On the 1962 record, John really started sounding like John. Getting more open in his phrasing. But if you compare that recording to the stuff with the NYC5 which is recorded only a year and a half later, it's amazing to hear how far he advanced in that time. He really was a lot more confident in his style."

In November of '63, John returned to New York while some of the other musicians stayed in Denmark for a while longer. However, once they were all back in New York, they hardly played together as a group any more, apart from a recording in early 1964 which was eventually released as the back side of an LP by the trumpeter Bill Dixon on the Savoy label. Maybe the group's moment had passed, John said later.

By then, John had started playing together intensively with trombonist Roswell Rudd. They'd had a connection since soon after he came to New York. Roswell described their first meeting: "Don Cherry said,

'You ought to go to this place in Midtown. A friend of mine from Europe is playing there, and I think you two guys would sound good together. Why don't you go and check it out?' So, I went up and I sat in with John. The combined sound of our playing is what I think captivated both of us. It just sounded good, right off."

Roswell had a background in Dixieland music, which contains a lot of collective improvisation, and he had a college education in music. He had transcribed a lot of the music of, for instance, Herbie Nichols, Duke Ellington, Billy Strayhorn and Thelonious Monk; he and the soprano saxophonist Steve Lacy had led a quartet which played only Monk's tunes. On the classical side, he was very familiar with Stravinsky and Ives.

John and Roswell spent much time practising together. Sometimes they played standards, but often they just started the music from scratch, beginning with a single note. One of them started and the other joined, just discovering how to make music together spontaneously. They wanted to have their improvisations based on melodies or melodic elements, but without set chords -- and not necessarily with a set form or a set rhythm or even a steady beat. Listening to each other -- "collective listening" -- was at the root of what became collective improvisation. The tenorist Booker Ervin, who came to prominence with Charles Mingus, later said about them in *Down Beat*: "... I heard a group in Denmark last year, John Tchicai and the trombone player Roswell Rudd, and sometimes it happened and sometimes it didn't. But when it happened, it was marvellous. They started out with something, and it happened to be a good melodic idea, [or] rhythmic idea, and they would elaborate on that, and after a while, they would get into things that sounded like, I guess... complete freedom, but still related to an essential idea. John is one of the most mature players in this kind of music."

Roswell mentioned a kind of telepathic contact between him and John when they were improvising, as if they knew what the other person was going to play before he played it. In an obituary for John, he wrote:

"We worked on getting a sound and gradually the music came. I emphasize sound because John had a very warm, original and instantly recognizable sound. What became the New York Art Quartet was his idea. We had some colorful musical experiences together, a few of which are documented. I feel I owe much of my musical inspiration at the time to John Tchicai's vision. His is a heavy loss."

There were no other rules than that you were supposed to listen to each other and use all your musical knowledge and experience in order to make it interesting. It felt good to both of them to do this.

The next step was to find a rhythm section and create a group, so they started practising together with different bassists and drummers. When it began to take shape, they held an open rehearsal at the loft of Michael Snow, a Canadian filmmaker who had just come to New York. Friends were invited to come and listen, and bring other friends with them. This is how they met the drummer Milford Graves, who had heard of the concert through a friend. John and Roswell played the first set as a quartet with bassist Don Moore and drummer J.C. Moses. For the second set, Milford took Moses' place. Milford was not a typical jazz drummer. He'd come from playing Cuban music, where percussion is in the foreground. He didn't play standard jazz rhythms but polyrhythms incorporating Cuban and African rhythms. It was a different approach from other jazz drummers, and John and Roswell loved it.

They felt it fitted exactly with what they had imagined, as John described it: "We had an intuitive kind of sense about what it was we wanted to do, and where we wanted to go, and that didn't happen before we found Milford Graves. He had this polyrhythmic ability. For me, that was just right up my alley. With Milford, it was the decisive step into the polyrhythmic world."

From then on they rehearsed with Milford and with different bassists and later, their group was called the New York Art Quartet, a name John came up with, helped by his artist friend Jan Telting.

John and Roswell composed themes and 'procedures' which were to be taken as guidelines. They wanted their music to be a combination of improvisation and composition. The form wasn't stuck to theme-improvisation-theme and the instrumental roles weren't the traditional ones where certain instruments always played solos and other instruments always played the accompaniment. Everybody could improvise and everybody was part of the rhythm section. Each player, setting his own line within the group, was responsible for the music as a whole. Rhythm and pulse were present in their music, but they were emphasized very differently than in traditional jazz. There was no steady rhythm, it wasn't always 1, 2, 3, 4 in a set tempo. Sometimes it was 1, 2, 1, 2, 3, sometimes it was faster or sometimes slower, and often there was no set tempo at all.

The melodic and soloistic aspect of the drums was much more prominent than in conventional forms of jazz. On the alto, John's playing became more than 'just' melodic or soloistic. He developed his way of playing ostinatos: melodic/rhythmic phrases that are repeated many times, sometimes given a different ending, sometimes played louder or softer, or stretched into a longer phrase. He improvised with these ideas to create structures around which the others could play, thereby anchoring the music. In that sense, John's playing sometimes adopted the role of a bass player or of a drummer. But there was no standard form. It was just music, a mixture of jazz, classical, Dixieland, Cuban and African sensibilities, and very far away from bebop. "The uniqueness of this group is the collective spirit," John said when they reunited in 1999. "Not like one person is up front and the other guys are backing up. "

According to the music journalist Ben Young, "The deeper the quartet got into what they did best, the more they drifted away from known audiences for improvised music, toward a no-man's land of sound with only a small constituency and no real lexicon to discuss what was going on."

A place where they could give their first official concert was hard to find with this unusual kind of music. The genre of non-traditional jazz seeking new forms was known by many names – free jazz, avant-garde jazz, the new thing – but it was hard to really explain what it stood for.

The only solution was to be able to play to people, allowing them to experience what it sounded like and define it for themselves.

Playing live was also an economic necessity. As John had discovered when he arrived on the Lower East Side, life was not easy for adventurous jazz musicians in the United States. At least he had his day job as a cook but that was irregular, too. Annette remembered "periods where we had $1 a day to spend on meals. Then John discovered curry powder, not known in Denmark before we left. He used it all the time. It was a cheap way to spice up the food."

Club owners and concert bookers were more inclined to book people who played the more straight-ahead jazz, because that was what people were used to, and it attracted bigger audiences. Players of "free jazz" had to resort to performances in small bars with small audiences. They were serious musicians and their music was interesting, but the difficulty of finding a place to play created intense frustration.

Jazz Composers' Guild meeting: L to R John Winter, Burton Greene, Bill Dixon, Sun Ra, Paul Bley, Roswell Rudd, Carla Bley, Mike Mantler, Cecil Taylor, John Tchicai, Archie Shepp. New York, 1964

In the summer of 1964, the trumpeter and composer Bill Dixon attempted to find an answer to the problem by organizing a union for the new generation of players. The intention was to create a strong collective voice that could be heard more clearly within society, could demand better working conditions and could give the musicians more control over their work. Dixon called it the Jazz Composers' Guild, and he invited other musicians to join. John became a member and so did Roswell Rudd, Archie Shepp, Paul Bley, Cecil Taylor, Sun Ra, Carla Bley and others. The Guild saw its members as "the most vital elements in the mainstream of America's contemporary musical culture", and they created a manifesto stating the following goals:

```
Jazz Composers' Guild goals:

1. (to) establish the music to its rightful place in
   the society;
2. (to) awaken the musical conscience of the masses of
   people to that music which is essential to their
   lives;
3. (to) protect the musicians and composers from the
   existing forces of exploitation and commerciality;
4. (to) provide an opportunity for the audience to hear
   the music;
5. (to) provide facilities for the proper creation,
   rehearsal and performance of the music.
```

One could say that the first goals are socially engaged but general and idealistic and the latter are more concrete. Dixon took a very concrete step by organising a festival at which musicians and audiences could get together. This festival took place at the Cellar Café on New York's Upper West Side in early October 1964 and was called the October Revolution in Jazz. For four nights in a row the member musicians could play there, with between four and seven groups per evening. The New York Art Quartet of John and Roswell's group with Milford had its first official concert there, albeit billed in the advertising material as the John Tchicai Quartet. Sun Ra led a sextet, Paul Bley a quintet, and the saxophonist Ken McIntyre an octet. Not all the musicians appearing were Guild members, but the leaders were.

The festival was a success. There were lines outside the Cellar Café of people waiting outside to get in, and there were good reviews in the newspapers and magazines. The Guild started organizing similar events once a month. The NYAQ played every time, which helped the group and their music to become known. The next time they were billed as the Roswell Rudd Quartet, but after that they performed under their final name.

During the last days of the year, the Guild organized a further four nights of concerts, this time at a larger venue, Judson Hall on Washington Square. New Years' Eve saw a double bill of the NYAQ and Sun Ra, now billed as "Le Sun Ra Arkestra". The printed program showed a short explanation of the music to help the listeners enjoy the music. Another concert in this same series was by the Jazz Composers' Orchestra, a large ensemble comprising members of the Guild playing compositions by other members. It was led by Carla Bley and Mike Mantler who provided most of the compositions.

According to Archie Shepp, "The Orchestra was more a performance platform for musicians and a way to perform rather than to control the works they'd written (as were the goals of the Guild). "

The monthly Guild presentations often had visuals in them. It could be film accompanied by live music. At one event, in April 1965, music and dance were joined together. John performed with Judy Dearing, combining an improvisation for alto saxophone with modern dance.

As these activities attracted more attention, a lawyer named Bernard Stollman became interested in recording and releasing the new music. He started the ESP-Disk label as a vehicle for avant-garde music, and he asked the NYAQ to record an LP with him. In November '64 they went into the studio.

Completing the quartet with John, Roswell and Milford on this date was Lewis Worrell, one of their regular bassists. "You could express yourself without worrying about being restricted by chords or anything like that," Worrell said. "We had a form, but you had to use your imagination... There was no need to 'advance the narrative'."

Also invited to this session was Amiri Baraka, who had emerged from the Greenwich Village beatnik scene of the 1950s to become a leading figure in the fight for civil rights. On one track he recited a long poem, accompanied by the band. Titled "Black Dada Nihilismus", it was a confrontational text which made no secret of its political viewpoint and attracted considerable attention.

New York Art Quartet: Roswell Rudd, John T, Milford Graves and Lewis Worrell. New York, 1964
©Marilyn Schwartz

In 1964 and '65, besides playing with and working to promote the NYAQ, John played on three other recording sessions which produced albums that attained classic status within the field of the new jazz. They were the ESP album *New York Eye & Ear Control*, Archie Shepp's *Four for Trane* and John Coltrane's *Ascension*.

New York Eye & Ear Control was the title of a film by Michael Snow, in whose loft John, Roswell and Milford had met. Snow wanted an ensemble to accompany his footage, improvising in a collective manner, with few solos. He invited John, Roswell, Don Cherry, Albert Ayler, Sunny Murray and Gary Peacock to take part, and on July 17, 1964 he recorded their playing in the loft of his neighbour Paul Haines, a poet, on Chambers Street in Lower Manhatten. Just over 40 minutes of playing were included on an LP which entered jazz history as one of the first recordings of an ensemble of younger players playing freely.

Four for Trane, recorded three weeks later, was the first product of Archie Shepp's deal with Impulse Records, a major label and the home of John Coltrane's recordings. Coltrane had introduced Shepp to Bob Thiele, the boss of Impulse, and produced the album himself, with the clear intention of introducing the new musicians to his own large audience. "I was very fortunate that I met John Coltrane," Shepp said. "He was very kind to me, and he made it possible for me to record the *Four for Trane* date. John Tchicai was on that one. Even though he and I didn't see each other as regularly as we had before, he remained one of my favorite saxophone players and I always found his musical voice very original."

This was a more formal affair than *New York Eye & Ear Control*. The four horns of Archie, John, Roswell and the trumpeter Alan Shorter, with Reggie Workman and Charles Moffett on bass and drums, recorded four Coltrane compositions plus a fifth piece by Shepp. More traditionally structured than the music John and Roswell were making with Milford, it took the form of theme-solos-theme, but it had openness, freshness and newness. It was music that existed on the edge of freedom, offering an entry point to listeners unfamiliar with what the new musicians were up to.

Charlie Kohlhase remembered John Tchicai telling him that Coltrane was very open towards young players. "He and others used to sit in when Coltrane's group was playing at the Half Note in New York. This is how Coltrane got to know young players that he later asked to play on his *Ascension* record date."

The famous *Ascension* session took place on June 28, 1965. Coltrane invited several musicians of the younger avant-garde set to join him in the Rudy Van Gelder's studio in New Jersey. John Tchicai and Archie Shepp were among them, along with the trumpeters Freddie Hubbard and Dewey Johnson, the altoist Marion Brown, the tenorist Pharoah Sanders and the members of Coltrane's regular rhythm section, the pianist McCoy Tyner, the bassist Jimmy Garrison and the drummer Elvin Jones, plus a second bassist, Art Davis. Coltrane showed them a chart that contained a few lines of music to be played together. In between the ensemble parts, each player had a solo where he could play as free as he liked. Two takes were recorded, the music bursting with energy and a sense of discovery. It was Coltrane's freest album to that point, and while it disconcerted some of his admirers, others were enthralled.

"Coltrane had a very original idea," Shepp said, "and for younger players like us it was an opportunity to really get our message out there." The album gave enormous exposure to the younger players like Tchicai. For the rest of his career, it became a regular question in interviews: "How was it to play with John Coltrane?" John replied that it was very impressive, and that there was such a great energy. When I once asked if he had any regrets concerning his career, he thought hard before replying he was sorry he hadn't made an album of his own with Coltrane. John had spoken with Coltrane about recording with the New York Art Quartet, and Coltrane was up for the idea. But it never came to pass. There were too many other plans, and perhaps not enough money, for it to come true before Coltrane's death in 1967 at the age of 40.

On July 2, 1965, a few days after the *Ascension* session, the Jazz Composer's Orchestra -- including John, Roswell and Milford -- played a set at the Newport Jazz Festival. This orchestra had performed at a few of the Guild events and the Newport appearance was their most prestigious gig so far. It gave everyone exposure to a larger audience. But something unpleasant happened that day which may have to do with the fact that the Jazz Composers' Guild would soon be no more. The musicians had to travel from New York City to the festival grounds on Rhode Island, and for several of them, who were black and poor, that wasn't easy to do. According to John, they had trouble finding a car and then got stopped on the way, so they arrived late. In his account, they were met by an angry Carla Bley. She might have been nervous, being the leader of that gig, but it was John's feeling that she had trouble understanding what life was for black musicians. I might paint it too harshly here, but racial differences may have played a role in the end of the Jazz Composers' Guild. The Orchestra continued in a different form. And so, though the Guild's goal was a very worthy cause, it went, in Archie Shepp's words, by the wayside. "For me," Shepp added, "I was offered a contract with Impulse, a major record company. It was a real opportunity. Unlike a number of the men and women who belonged to the Guild, I was married at the time and had three children. So I had to make a choice between surviving and hopefully moving my career along, and remaining in the society, where there was not really much from a commercial point of view. "

John played with the Jazz Composers' Orchestra for the last time on July 15 at MoMA, the Museum of Modern Art in New York City. The orchestra opened the concert, and the second set was played by the NYAQ, with Reggie Workman on bass. At the museum he liked so much, John wanted to make a visual artistic statement. He painted his face. This was not something that jazz musicians did, although few years later it was taken up by members of the Art Ensemble of Chicago. John painted his face in the style of the very distinctive portraits that Dutch artist Marte Röling had made for a series of albums of avant-garde jazz issued by the Fontana label in Holland. One of those albums was the New York Contemporary Five's *Consequences*, for which she had painted the heads of Archie Shepp, Don Cherry and John, whom she gave a yellow ear.

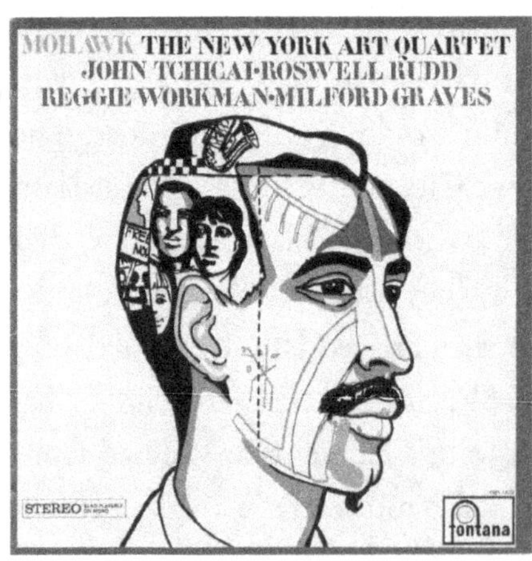

Mohawk, NYAQ's second LP, design by Marte Röling, 1965

"I met John twice and I remember apologizing to him about giving him a yellow ear," Marte Röling said. "He laughed and said he didn't mind. I liked John a lot and I liked his music, too. "

On the day after the MoMA concert, the NYAQ went into Rudy Van Gelder's studio in Englewood Cliffs, New Jersey to record their second album. This time they included no poetry, but

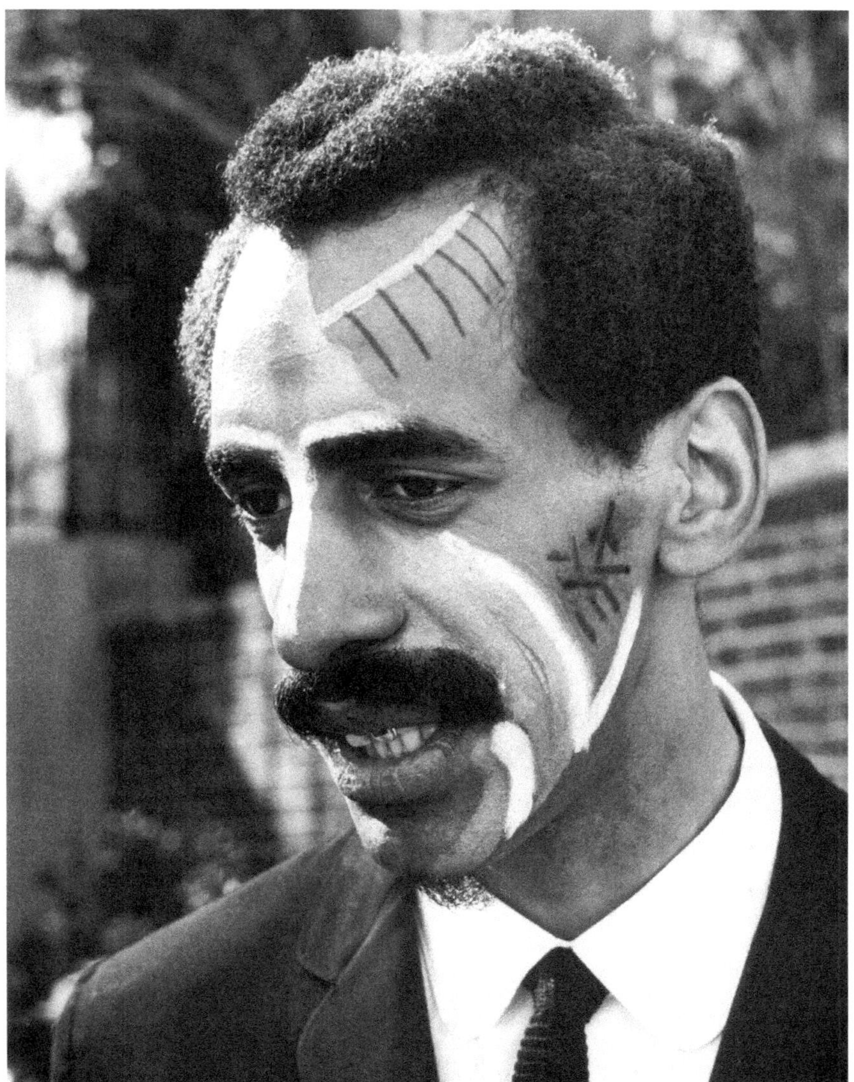

John's face painting. New York, 1965
©Raymond Ross Archives/CTSIMAGES

along with their own compositions they recorded a standard ballad, "Everything Happens to Me", and the Charlie Parker composition, "Mohawk", which gave the album its title. John's "Quintus T" was named after his friend Jan Quintus Telting, the Surinamese artist, while the title of Roswell's "Banging on the White House Door" fitted the insurrectionary mood of the times. *Mohawk* came out on Fontana in October; this time John's head was the only one on the cover, and again Marta Röling had painted his ear yellow.

In his liner notes, John wrote: "There is so much talk about the *freedom* of this music, but the musicians still have to abide to the rules of artistical responsibility, and they should never forget that whichever way the technique develops: the content (the feeling) must always be there (passion, energy, lyric, strength)."

The next day, John and Annette went to Denmark for vacation and for what John had hoped would be be a European tour for the NYAQ. But it was difficult to get all musicians over from the USA. John was full of energy and could be impatient. On July 26, hardly a week after his departure from NYC, he wrote to Roswell, saying, "What's happening to you man? Why is there still no answer from you?" Even if Roswell had written, a letter from New York could hardly have arrived in Denmark yet.

In the end Roswell was the only one to come over for a short tour. It was billed as the New York Art Quartet, and the group was completed by the South African drummer Louis Moholo and the Danish bassist Finn von Eyben. They played in Denmark, Belgium and Holland. There, in the Hague and Amsterdam, they shared the bill with Ornette Coleman's trio.

Back in Copenhagen, they gathered a group of Danish musicians to record some of Roswell's compositions for large ensemble. Pianist Jørn-Erik Jensen, John's old friend from Aarhus, was involved, but the recording was never released.

While in Denmark, John had other musical meetings that proved to be important for him. Louis Moholo, for example, was a member of the Blue Notes, a group of South African musicians who had come to Europe in 1964 to play at the Antibes Jazz Festival and were subsequently exiled from their country. The bassist Johnny Dyani and the pianist Chris McGregor were two more of the group staying in Denmark at the time. Later in his career John got to play a lot with these musicians. He invited Moholo to play a concert with him on August 1 in Comblain-la-Tour, Belgium, where he met two young German musicians exploring the possibilities of free jazz, the saxophonist Peter Brötzmann and the bassist Peter Kowald.

John also met his idol, the altoist Lee Konitz, who was now living in Denmark. They became friends and played together often, inside apartments or outside in the parks. John's mother Ketty invited Lee to come for dinner at her house. On the back of a photo Lee gave her, he wrote a warm dedication. John told me he'd taken lessons with Lee. He always remained fascinated with the way Lee played. There's a photo of John and Roswell with Lee Konitz on stage, taken on the opening night of their NYAQ tour in 1965, when Lee sat in with them.

John worked hard on the promotion of his music and the advancement of his career in a world where young jazz musicians received little attention from the mainstream newspapers, magazines, television and radio stations. He was never shy about asking journalists to review the albums in which he was involved.

Jazzmagazine Downbeat, February 1966

Little by little, John became better known and in February 1966 he received the accolade of a cover story in *Down Beat*, the leading American jazz magazine.

This article was an interview by Dan Morgenstern, whose phrase to describe John -- "a quiet member of the avant-garde" – became the headline on the magazine's cover. In the interview, John elaborated on his views on the Jazz Composers' Guild and on racial differences in music.

"There's no use in getting discouraged," he said. "You've got to try to do the best you can. I hate to give up what I have decided to do. It always takes a little work if you want something… Whether you're a black or a white artist, if you're playing the new music that people haven't been exposed to, it's obvious that you'll meet a lot of resistance, and can't fall back and blame it all on the black and white thing. The music doesn't have any color. You can't see music, so how can you give it a color? The word 'jazz' is just a label, I would prefer to call what I play simply 'music'. "

John sometimes asked musicians if they wanted to do collaborations. One of them was the arranger Gil Evans, an older man who had created the highly successful albums *Miles Ahead*, *Porgy & Bess* and *Sketches of Spain* for Miles Davis and was known for his open-minded approach to music. John asked him to arrange one of his compositions. Evans agreed but it never came about.

Hoping to land a contract with a major label, John contacted John Hammond, the celebrated and idealistic A&R man who had been involved with Count Basie and Billie Holiday in the 1930s and had signed Bob Dylan to Columbia Records in the early '60s. In February 1966, John received a letter from Hammond, saying it was unfortunate but it would not be possible. "With John Handy, Prince Lasha and Charles Lloyd, we are pretty well staffed with alto players and experimentation in jazz," Hammond wrote. "I was very, very interested in meeting you and I do hope that there will be sometime in the future when we can get together. It just happens that you came around at the wrong time for any immediate release here at Columbia."

Keen to pursue the NYAQ project, John imagined them living together in one house and working constantly to develop the music. He had tried to organise a college tour throughout the US, believing that there, he could find audiences who were open to new music -- and also decent money and organization. He contacted Ornette Coleman, Lee Konitz, John Coltrane and Ali Akbar Khan to see if they were interested in sharing a double bill project with them. Ornette wrote back:

May 14, 1966

Dear John,
I got your letter and I hope you do the things you wish with your music
career, if I can help in any way, it would please me very much. In your
letter, you wrote about a college package-tour. Well, if you get it to happen
for yourself or anyone in the States, it will be just great without the USA-
bookers' hands in it. I will quote you a price. About the lowness of prices,
forget it, as far I am concerned. If you and I or anyone play for an audience
and they come to hear you, only that should have anything to do with wages
for performing now. For me, I will not take under 1500$ for an audience of
500 to 800 - our pay over note 1500 to 2500, if you can get these wages for
yourself or anyone I'll go along with the program, if not the only other way I
would do it for less, is that I would be offered not less than 12 concerts
within 2 weeks at 1000$ a concert with all traveling paid to and from each
concert. I hope I do not give you the wrong idea about my wants. But I do
hope you will understand that I am only saying I don't want to save any
money for anyone first but the musicians, if someone can make money with
me performing for them that is fine but I don't wish to perform just to save
someone some money who is just getting the money from the audience. It
isn't the same if someone pays you and no people show up, so if the college
can open a way for us musicians I'm all for that, but John count me out if
you are trying to save money for some booker. You can write me at the
American Express in London if you wish to write a reply to this letter or if
you just want to write anything concerning your ideas about the music-
business. Take care and stay as healthy and happy as you can.

Ornette

The college tour never happened. John's plans and hopes were bigger than he could realize so quickly. And already the quartet's members were going off in different directions.

In the *Down Beat* interview, John also said he thought he had grown beyond making music to be played in a bar or club where people were eating, drinking and talking at the same time. "This music is crystallizing," he said. "It needs attentive listening. It's not background music, and ideally, it should be presented in concert halls or in a new kind of club, where people can sit quietly."

To translate these words into deeds, he organized a concert at Carnegie Recital Hall in New York City. He rented the hall for an evening in June in order to present his extended composition titled *Scandinavian Discoveries*, written for a jazz quartet plus string quartet. The score was written on a scroll of nine A3-sized sheets of paper glued together, four metres long. Mostly written in regular notation, it also included John's use of little designs and drawings.

The Dutch pianist Piet Kuiters came over from Europe specially for the concert, but the performance was not generally well received. A *New York Times* review was not very positive, and it seems the musicians may not have had a great deal of time to rehearse. John did not discard the piece, however, and a few years later he recorded it with Dutch musicians for the VARA radio station, part of the Netherlands' public broadcasting network. The score remains among his papers.

By the time of the concert, John was on his way out of New York City. Annette's contract at the Danish Consulate had ended and they were heading back to Copenhagen. They packed up their stuff, sent part of it off on the boat to Denmark, and left the rest in storage. The idea was it would only be a temporary departure from the US. But once they were back in Denmark, so many things happened that John didn't return to New York for a number of years.

"Good morning John."

"Good morning, sweetie. Hey, I have an idea for a new project. We can play this and this music with those and those people in that and that city, you know, by late summer. Wouldn't that be great? Maybe this or that guy would like to present it."

"Yes, that sounds good."

Half an hour later: "Can you type out this letter here and send it off with these materials here in them? I just called him and he says he wants to see a little text about it before deciding."

Forty minutes later: "I called these musicians and they're cool, they're up for it. And I called Fred but he wasn't there, so I left a message on his machine. - I'm going to select the charts so we can send them off."

A few hours later, letters were taken to the post office, charts were sent off. Messages were left on answering machines with other possible participants or organizers. Then John left for a little walk in nature. Coming back in, the first question was: "Did Fred call back? No? Hmm. Maybe tomorrow."

Two days later, Fred hadn't called or written back yet. "Strange. Why doesn't he call back?"

"Perhaps he hasn't gotten the letter yet."

"Oh? Yeah...."

A few more days later, Fred, perhaps living in a different state or country, called and the phone rang: "Oh yeah, hi! Listen it's about ....." John explained the plan.

It was hard for him to wait. If you asked John for help, he also helped you right away. But not everybody reacted that way, and if they called a week or a few weeks later, sometimes John's plans had already changed.

That's how I experienced John when I first met him. Then he was in his fifties. When he was younger, he must have had an unstoppable drive in order to realize his ideas and projects and get his music out to the world.

BACK TO DENMARK

In July 1966, John returned to Denmark. His reputation at home had grown through his collaborations with the likes of John Coltrane, Archie Shepp and Roswell Rudd, and through his tours with the New York Contemporary 5 and the New York Art Quartet. Now he was 30 years old and full of energy and ambition to realize, develop and promote his music and to have it fully accepted within the Danish musical society.

After three and a half years in New York, living in Denmark required adjustment. The Danish culture seemed a bit slow and stale

Back in Copenhagen, 1966
©Teit Jørgensen

to John, even though the Sixties were in full swing with some aspects of society shaking and changing. He tried to get in touch with other creative musicians, photographers, filmmakers, painters, artists and other hippies, and took part in 'happenings': spontaneous, improvised performances with a combination of different art forms, later known as 'performance art'.

For instance, besides playing the saxophone, John might have to play a certain role as in a happening with poet Ted Joans, or to wear a certain costume created by Swedish artist Moki Karlsson. She designed stage

Happening with Don and Moki Cherry. Copenhagen, 1967
©Teit Jørgensen

and costumes for John, her husband the trumpeter Don Cherry, other friends and herself.

John met his old friend Niels Holt again, the activist/saxophonist/critic/philosopher who had introduced him to jazz when he was 14. "I saw John again one day, when he was playing in one of these houses we had squatted," Niels said. "I was a member of several teams who squatted buildings and changed them into meeting places for young people.

We had weekly meetings in my apartment in Copenhagen. It was very big, six rooms, and 200 metres from the central train station. An awful lot of people came there: many people I didn't know, many musicians I didn't know. I went through a scrapbook one day and was very surprised when I saw the names of all these people, because if you go through an album of records, then practically everyone of those who produced records in that period came to my apartment."

Right away John was busy. In October 1966 he did a performance for Danish Radio and in December he had a trip abroad to Holland for a tour with two Dutch musicians, the pianist Misha Mengelberg and the drummer Han Bennink, who would become leading members of the Amsterdam-based Instant Composers Pool. They had heard him play in Amsterdam the year before and they established a steady connection for several years.

In between he played within Denmark with other experimental musicians to see if they could work together. Very soon he formed a steady group with musicians, including the trumpeter Hugh Steinmetz and the altoist Karsten Vogel. They practised regularly and formed a group which became known as Cadentia Nova Danica ("New Danish Cadence"). Starting out as a double-quartet in the style of Ornette Coleman's *Free Jazz* recording, the group included two bassists, two drummers, two alto saxophones, and two brass (a trumpet and a trombone) and it lasted, through various personnel changes, until 1971.

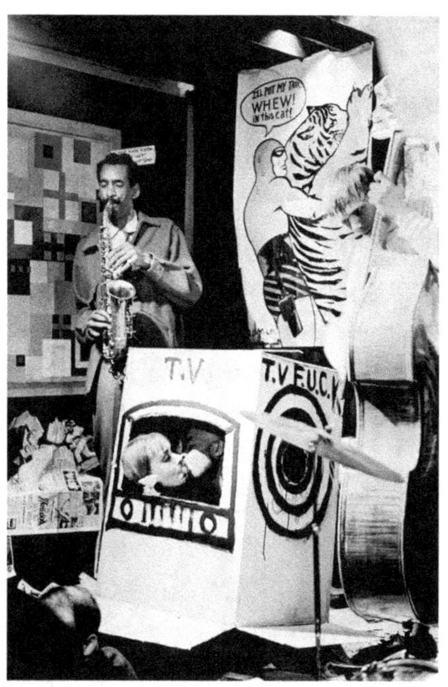

Happening with trumpeter Ted Joans.
Copenhagen, 1966
©Teit Jørgensen

In those days, photocopiers were not yet available so John wrote the copies of his charts for each of his fellow musicians by hand, in felt-tip pen. Sometimes he used pens of different colors in order to indicate an interaction between the various instruments.

"It was composed music in a very free environment," Karsten Vogel said. "John called it 'Komponist Udøver Ensemble', which means something like "Performing Composers' Orchestra". So the composition-part was very important for him. The music was free when you played the solo: there were no chord changes you had to follow, and there was no 'four beats in the bar' that you had to follow. You had to follow the idea of the composer's composition, in that particular song. John wrote most compositions in the beginning. I had a few."

It took a while before they found promoters willing to book them, but by July '67, when they were invited to play at the Molde Jazz Festival in Norway, it had started to take off. A video recording of their Molde set shows John with a bald head and a very serious look on his face. Piet Kuiters, who had gone to New York to play on *Scandinavian Discoveries*, sat in with them on piano that day.

In August they played at the Jazzhus Montmartre, a recording of which was only released on CD many years later. The compositions were contributed by different band members: two by John, one by Karsten, and even one piece by Misha Mengelberg. The recording shows that John's use of ostinatos had changed: now he didn't only play them himself as part of the improvisation, but he was also writing them out to be played by other instruments, making them an integral part of some of his compositions. "In the jazz area in Denmark at least, John was the first," Vogel said. "But also worldwide, he was among the first musicians to make free music over ostinatos."

And on October 1, 1967, when rock guitarist and composer Frank Zappa led the Mothers of Invention into the Falconer Salen for their first Copenhagen concert in their first European tour, Cadentia Nova Danica played the opening set: a sign of the convergence of young jazz and rock musicians towards the end of the decade. After that high-profile show, the number of opportunities increased. The group also played at places where people usually came to dance to pop music. They found that audiences listened to what they were doing, and liked it.

A year after their return from New York, and after almost ten years of living together, John and Annette went their separate ways. He was working hard to promote his own music, wanting that to be the career that provided his income, without having to go back to cooking in restaurants.

To raise some money, he tried to sell the second, unreleased part of the New York Contemporary Five recordings made in Copenhagen four years earlier and still lying on the shelf. When he found that Fontana were willing to put it out, he was blocked by Archie Shepp, who threatened legal action unless he received a larger payment. John was unable to obtain the extra money. Some time later, however, the recordings were finally released, the music of what had been a co-operative group now credited to "Archie Shepp and the New York Contemporary Five".

For a while, John worked as a postman to make ends meet. He took his music, and music in general, very seriously and he believed his work should get the same respect as that of musicians in the classical field. So he wrote to organizers and institutions that helped classical music, asking them to help his music as well. But support from that quarter was frustratingly difficult to obtain. Official organisations often didn't consider John's music as valuable, perhaps because it was so new and different.

Usually, John was a calm, serious person, but he was strong and could get impatient. In January 1968 there was a dramatic scene at the Danish Radio studios in Copenhagen. After meeting with somebody about not getting a radio recording, John became so exasperated and angry that in the middle of the studio's cafeteria, he threw his saxophone on the floor and trampled on it. Then he took a tray full of glasses from a rack and threw it on the floor, too, and did the same with another tray, while shouting: "This is how Denmark deals with new music and with musicians who don't play like everybody else!" Then he left.

Niels Holt, John's old friend and a fellow saxophonist, lived close to the studios and recalled the incident. "John was a strange character when he was young," he said. "I remember him going to the radio house and smashing his saxophone onto the floor. He came to me right after and asked if he could borrow my alto, because he'd just smashed his. He wasn't shocked or angry. I said, yes, of course. He used mine for many, many years."

Cadentia Nova Danica finally did get a recording session and their music was broadcast on the radio. And in 1969 John was chosen as the country's "Jazz Musician of the Year" by the Danish Jazz Circle.

One of John's non-musician friends was Stuart Fox, an American photographer/filmmaker. Stuart had fled his country and given up his citizenship to avoid military service in the Vietnam war. He became a Danish citizen instead. With Stuart and Niels Holt, John started a multimedia event called *Skumgummipindsvin* (Foam rubber porcupine), performed in a theatre in a combination of photography, film and music.

"We were standing behind a white screen that we projected the images on," Niels Holt remembered. "John and five or six musicians were behind the screen. We could see the image, because it shone through, and we were standing there, improvising. Sometimes John would do what he often did, play a little banal melody from a children's music book or whatever, just a little thing in between, so that people would hear this little theme come through. This was something that Mahler also did in his work, and John had heard all these records at my place, the classical records, and we talked about it a lot. We had *Skumgummipindsvin* events for several years. "

Stuart Fox played a role in Cadentia Nova Danica's first trip to the UK for a pair of concerts in October of 1968. They travelled by train through Germany and Holland before boarding the ferry to England. That day, there was heavy weather in the English channel, and two of the players got seasick. To help them put their minds on something else, the group held an impromptu rehearsal on the car deck.

They had a well-received concert in London in a sold-out Wigmore Hall, a historic venue where chamber music was usually performed. The evening was organised by the percussionist/poet Anthony Barnett, who later became a musician in Cadentia Nova Danica himself. In Manchester, by contrast, they had been invited to play at a trade fair. For them, it was by no means a typical musical experience. On a stand at the fair, the

Danish dairy products board was displaying Fox's photographs of Danish cows and landscapes to promote their dairy products. The members of Cadentia Nova Danica provided a musical accompaniment.

On a lucky day, John met Marianne Lassen who was a visual artist working with painting, pictures and textiles. Among other things, she sewed a beautiful garment for John to perform in, as well as a textile instrument holder for his growing collection of bamboo flutes which he used for many years. Marianne had two young children: Anders, a boy, and Stine, a girl. John moved in with them.

"We lived in a house in Gentofte," Anders remembered. "John and Marianne painted a tall 'OM' sign on the outside wall. It's taken down now to be a parking lot. John often took us to second-hand shops. He knew several places and people there knew him, they called him by his first name. We often bought records there, old 45 or 78 discs. We washed them with regular dishwashing liquid and dried them in the dish rack. Then we listened to them and marked each side: green for a good side and red for a bad side. Jimi Hendrix got a green mark. John often took me with him when he had to go to the Danish Radio studio. I had to be silent when the red light was on: recording! I still like the sound of a big band because of these visits."

His sister Stine recalled: "I earned respect from my classmates, being brought to school on a scooter by a tall, black man wearing a leather jacket and a cap. He had a white Vespa with colorful spots all over it."

In May '68, when flower power activities and demonstrations were putting regular life on hold throughout western Europe, John played a concert with Han Bennink and Misha Mengelberg in Amsterdam. In Hamburg, he did a recording session for NDR, a German radio station, with the pianist Dollar Brand, the saxophonist Gato Barbieri, the bassist Barre Philips and the drummer Makaya Ntshoko. Back in Denmark, he took part in a benefit concert for Amiri Baraka, who had been arrested during the civil rights uprising in Newark, New Jersey. John, who had once appeared at a Black Panther event in Copenhagen, now played with Dexter Gordon's Quartet at Jazzhus Montmartre to raise money for Baraka's defense.

Copenhagen, ±1969

He was still hanging out with other artists at Niels Holt's loft. "We all smoked weed," Holt said. "We were all turning on before playing, everyone – John, too. But he got on this Indian trip at a certain time and so he stopped, simply because of that." Marianne and John were both interested in yoga and Eastern religion, and John started taking yoga lessons.

Following the success of Cadentia Nova Danica's London concert, Anthony Barnett asked John to come back a few months later, for an event billing itself as 'the first international avant-garde concert of fundamentally improvised music and open sound in England', to be held at Cambridge University on March 2, 1969. The line-up of this "concert-workshop" was impressive: there were some of the South African musicians in exile (Johnny Dyani, Louis Moholo, Chris McGregor), other international players like the saxophonists Willem Breuker and Peter Bennink from Holland, the bassist Barre Philips who was an American expatriate in France, and more.

John suggested to Anthony that the audience should be encouraged to bring small percussion instruments with them. Half-jokingly, he also suggested that an invitation should be sent to the Japanese artist Yoko

Ono, who had performed as a singer with Ornette Coleman's group the year before. Once associated with the Fluxus group of experimental artists in New York, now she was living in London, where Barnett had made her acquaintance. Ono agreed to perform, but said she wanted to bring her own band. To general surprise, that turned out to be her new boyfriend John Lennon, who was still officially a member of the Beatles. They arrived in a white Rolls Royce bringing a guitar and amplifier, recording equipment, roadies and technicians.

The original plan of the concert was that everyone was free to play together in groupings they would sort out for themselves as the concert progressed, but the new arrivals had other ideas. It was decided on the spot that the other musicians would begin and that they would stop to make space for Ono and Lennon. When it was their turn, Ono began screaming loudly and Lennon held his guitar in front of the amplifier to make feedback sounds, while at the side of the stage an alarm clock was ticking. After about twenty minutes of this, John Tchicai and the drummer John Stevens returned to the stage and began playing with them. Others also came back and joined in. The concert went on, musicians and a few audience members were playing, but Ono and Lennon stopped. They left the stage to what the journalist and photographer Val Wilmer described as "a notable lack of applause" while their technicians unplugged cables. Before the concert was over, their Rolls Royce had left Cambridge.

For Lennon, this occasion was the first time he had played anything else than the Beatles' repertoire in public. In a sense, he had come out of the closet that day. Right away, he and Ono wanted to release an LP of the recording their technicians had made. *Unfinished Music No 2: Life with Lions* came out two months later. John Tchicai can be heard adding melody to their set. In an indirect way he was asked for his permission, and he gave it, but he -- who was later described by Lennon as "apparently a famous avant-garde sax guy"

John Lennon's
thank you note to
John Tchicai

-- never received an offer of money. All he got was one copy of the record, with a thank-you note and a drawing on the inner sleeve, in Lennon's handwriting.

John Tchicai is almost certainly the only musician who recorded with both John Coltrane and John Lennon.

Soon after the Cambridge concert, in April 1969, John decided to explore the possibilities of a large ensemble. He had been listening to a lot of different music, from classical composers -- Bartok, Stravinsky, Prokofiev, Schönberg, Webern and more -- to music from India and Africa, and now he wanted to create a jazz symphony orchestra.

He put an ad in a Danish jazz magazine, saying everybody was welcome to come to the Reprise Teatret, a cinema north of Copenhagen that presented a concert series called *Jazz i Reprisen*. John performed about ten concerts there in 1969. For this new project, there was a rehearsal on Saturday morning, followed by a performance open to the public in the afternoon. Pierre Dørge joined right away. He'd first seen John play when he was a young kid, and after seeing Cadentia Nova Danica play at the Jazzhus Montmartre the winter before, his interest had grown stronger. John had been playing a big marching-band drum on stage.

Pierre had liked it a lot: "At that concert, John was playing on that big bass drum and the others were playing some ostinato and there was a very powerful rhythm section and I loved the themes. It was really a great experience for me, opening my ears in some other directions. So now we were about 40 musicians showing up and there were some musicians that had just bought some Moroccan clay drums in some of these hippie shops, Indian clothes shops, you know, or somebody had been playing the recorder for three weeks, flute or penny whistle or anything. Some had trumpets and I had my electric guitar and there was a bass player, Steffen Andersen, who was playing with Cadentia Nova Danica already, and Hugh Steinmetz was there, the trumpet player that worked with John.

"And then we played some. John played something and we imitated, so we learned a few lines and we also got some written notes, just one line of notes with a lot of small things written to it, a full page. It was very, very exciting and this approach went directly to my heart, and then there were all these amateurs and half-professionals... John would lead on his alto and then everybody followed his voice and it was like a giant pencil painting. It was not in tune, but there were so many different tunings, there was almost half a note in between the tunings you know, so it sounded fantastic and then John was leading the melody... (Pierre sings a few ascending notes) Some played a little too high and some played a little too low and some played wrong on a recorder and some would play the bongo at a rhythm that was so far away from what was happening... It was like a boat in high sea, very chaotic, but I loved it. And then suddenly, he was looking at you and you should improvise, you know, or this group or this instrument should improvise. John didn't say very much and I was still very shy. He was not a person that you would talk to and ask a question, not with so many people around. I didn't want to raise my hand and ask 'What do you mean by this?' or something. Just follow the leader you know.

"We had a rehearsal at 10 or 11 o'clock, and at two o'clock there was a performance, from two till four o'clock. There was also a guest who was in town and John knew him. It was Lee Konitz. He was there, listening."

After that first performance, they got together twice a month.

Workshops were becoming a part of John's life. In 1968 he was invited to Vallekilde summer high school, a cultural training center in West-Sjælland. During the week, the attendees would practise their music and at the weekend they would perform it. John taught there for many years, leading the students in performances on the lawn and in parades among the trees of the center.

He applied successfully for a grant to do a project at normal schools and got it, so he took a group with Han Bennink, Misha Mengelberg,

Pierre Dørge and Steffen Andersen on visits to schools in and around Copenhagen. They played 21 concerts in one week, that means three concerts per day: an intense experience for improvising musicians.

"When I played free jazz," Pierre Dørge said, "it was as if my whole body was screaming, building something up to a climax. You start very slowly, and you build up and then there's an explosion. Suddenly for me to do this three times a day was like, 'What is this?' I found out that at the second concert in the morning at a new school, I couldn't do it every time with that full power. That was my first experience in feeling that you play on routine. But actually, when I heard recordings of it later, I heard the second concert was as good as the first one. It was just my inner feeling that was different because there was still full power and awareness of what was happening.

"Playing with Han and Misha was like an adventure, especially Han was unbelievable. He played a conch-shell trumpet, he made his own drums, he used cat intestine strings on a drum and was playing them with thin sticks that you use for pot plants or flowers. You could buy them at a garden shop. Every time he would buy 100 of these sticks because he would smash them all the time. But to be close to John, his sounds and his charisma was so inspiring to me, it was just a fantastic situation. I didn't really know what was happening, I was just following into his universe."

Han Bennink noted John's effect on the musicians around him: "There were many good players in Denmark at that time, but you could hear they were all influenced by John. I loved John's sound on alto and on soprano. John taught me something to play on the sopranino sax that I still play to this day."

A few months after that, John went to Holland and recorded with Han and Misha for the first albums made with their Instant Composers Pool group. The idea that improvisers were composers, too, was clearly alive in other parts of the world.

Han remembered John as a usually very quiet person who could sometimes burst out in anger. For instance when they were on a tour in

Holland with Derek Bailey and others, and about to go into a restaurant, all of a sudden John got very mad with Derek on the subject of food. "Perhaps for him, with his training as a chef, eating fish and chips several days in a row was something he really didn't like doing."

• In July 1969, Cadentia Nova Danica finally had an official recording date, and for this occasion they used a large ensemble of 22 people. Pierre Dørge was one of the musicians from the Saturday sessions who was asked to participate in this recording. Other players included Willem Breuker, J.C.Moses, John's old friend Max Brüel, John's brother Mauritz on the sousaphone, and more. They recorded three compositions by John and one 20-minute piece by Hugh Steinmetz called "Afrodisiaca" as well as a march-like song arranged by John called "This is Heaven". The session took place three days before Neil Armstrong landed on the moon. *Afrodisiaca* became the title of the album, with a typically late'60s cover of John and his family posing in the nude.

At around the same time, Cadentia Nova Danica finally won a contract to appear regularly on the national radio station. "We played four months in the fall and four months in the springtime, and every one of us got paid," Pierre Dørge remembered. "At that time we were about 20 people in the group. We were paid for one rehearsal a week and for making the programme, and that was like a worker's full fee for one month. It was like 1700 or 1800 kroner and in those days that was a lot of money. I remember the same year, a schoolteacher's monthly salary was 2500 and this was like 1800, so this was very high."

The group also collaborated with composers who normally worked in a more classical vein and who were looking for experimental situations. Their recordings included one in the Nørreport subway station, where they incorporated the chimes that announced the closing of the train doors into their music. The musicians were supposed to take each time the chimes sounded as a cue to play a specific line in a composition. Another session was at a fairground, where the musicians sat in a carousel and played while it was spinning around. The microphones

John leading a music parade in a Copenhagen park. 1970
©Jens Jørn Gjedsted

were located at fixed points, so you could hear each player become louder and softer as he came by. Sometimes, too, John would gather a large number of musicians in a park and set off for a parade through the center of Copenhagen, playing their instruments as they went.

John also did occasional solo concerts and in 1970 was even in an opera broadcast on television. Classical musicians mounted Alban Berg's opera "Lulu" and they asked John to perform a part in it. John liked it because he was interested in that music and he wanted to develop his voice. But in the end his voice was dubbed by someone else and he wrote: "My hope fell into the background."

John had been taking driving lessons and exchanged his Vespa scooter for a car. He bought a big Volvo and together with Marianne and the two children, Anders and Stine, he went on a long camping trip to the island Krk in Yugoslavia. They went via Montreux, where John played a concert at the festival, and Venice where he had a few musician friends.

"With John, we played music on everything we could find," Anders said. "If we saw wood logs stacked in a forest, John played it like it was a xylophone. On water, he played, too, slapping it with his flat hands. I remember he had a performance where all musicians were wearing bird masks. They were made by Misha Mengelberg's wife." This must have been part of *Ornithology*, a film project by Han Bennink and Misha Mengelberg. It was filmed in the forest and the musicians were dressed up as birds.

4

RETREATING

At home, John and Marianne, who both had strong temperaments, sometimes clashed. They were already doing yoga and meditation and they came to think that serious spiritual training, guided by a guru, could help them better control their minds and moods. In 1970, Marianne found guru Swami Narayanananda, an Indian yogi who had come to Denmark. Together they went to his sessions. John liked it a lot and soon underwent an official 'initiation' which gave him a new name, Jnanapriyananda. He wrote about this journey at the time: "I'm interested in finding the genuine source of life in myself and the genuine source of music. I think those two considerations are tied up very much. I have certain spiritual beliefs about human beings, and the best place to find these sources of music are to look into the yoga and Zen teachings."

That year he performed a concert in a church in Copenhagen and he wrote an extensive explanation in the programme of why it was important to play their music in a spiritual center instead of in a club. And when on a tour in Holland, he noted in his calendar that he "picked up (guru) Satchidananda from the airport with (pianist) Burton Greene, and did a meditation with him at Kosmos" -- a new-age center in Amsterdam.

The guru's community started an ashram in Jutland, south of Aarhus. John was so much into it that he asked the members of Cadentia Nova Danica to join him in the ashram "in order to become an even better working unit". If everybody lived there, it would be beneficial to them and to their music. They couldn't play their regular instruments but instead they could do a lot of singing and use bells and small percussion. For most of the musicians that was too much to ask, and Cadentia Nova Danica, one of the most important groups of its era on the European new music scene, fell apart.

Instead John tried to put together an ensemble within the ashram, finding people through a message on the notice board which said that formal musical knowledge was not needed. He found a small group of people and played devotional music with them.

The guru and his Danish helpers who led daily life in the ashram had a strong influence on the followers. The ashram started a school where adherents could send their children, to give them a better spiritual education. Marianne's children went to this boarding school. She and John were married on the guru's instigation; he told them that living together while unmarried wasn't good. And then, when they were married, he said that for a good spiritual training they shouldn't have sex. Of course that wasn't simple to live with.

John felt that to pursue his spiritual practice he couldn't go on with his music career. Instead, he became a teacher at a school nearby that gave a lot of attention to culture and the arts, where he taught music to all classes, with children from six to 16 years old. He also led the school choir and started an ensemble with some of the teachers. John got very involved and went with classes on a school excursion to Sweden. He asked for a piano in his classroom.

In this period, he gave hardly any other concerts. When he did play with old friends, it seems to have been more for fun than for an economic reason. He often listened to radio broadcasts and recorded some of them with his reel to reel tape recorder. He also enlarged his collection of albums. But he was mostly busy with the school, the family and the spiritual training. Notes about the yoga and meditation exercises he was doing were entered in his appointments diary. He set up a disciplined routine that he kept for the rest of his life.

But although the temperament problems at home were reduced, the stress of ashram life weighed too heavily on John and Marianne. They split up in 1973. From then on, John lived in celibacy for several years.

At the school, John developed his teaching methods, creating a combination of singing, clapping and playing small percussion on a similar set of instruments that he was using in his ashram ensemble. The children sang Danish folk songs and other folk music, and played songs using Orff instruments – a set of tuned percussion of varying sizes. But John also devised improvisation games and exercises with them, and he stimulated them to compose small melodies and rhythms.

Sometimes he even encouraged them with money. An entry in his diary says: "50 øre for three different rhythms per person; 50 øre for the best bell player or for the best drummer (hand drums)." He recorded the results, and he also performed school concerts with the children. Colleague music teacher Bodil Høyer remembers an event in the school hall with birds singing and children singing and playing, and a very enthusiastic, creative atmosphere.

Sometimes he taught workshops at adult summer schools like the one in Vallekilde. He taught there for instance a week-long workshop

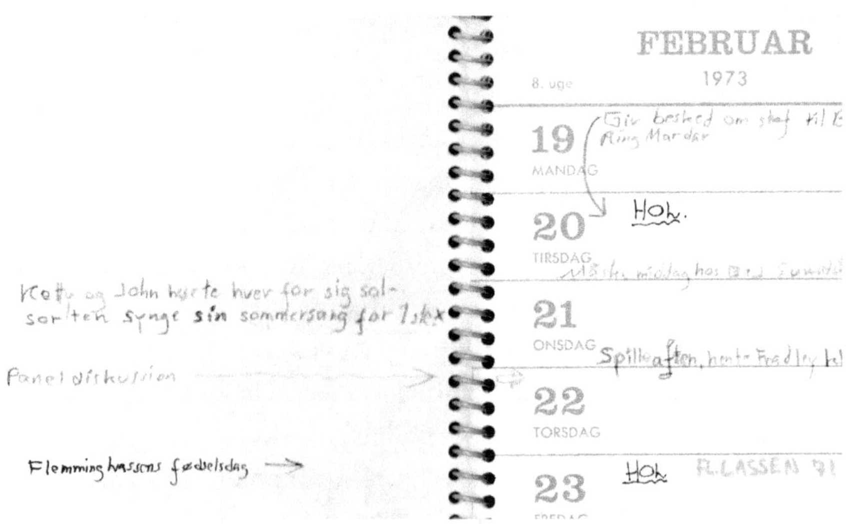

Note in John's appointment diary: "(Mother) Ketty and I both, but each on his own, heard the blackbird sing its summer song for the 1st time"

in *'Spontaneous musikudfoldelse for kvinde og mandstemmer'* (spontaneous music development for women's and men's voices). It could involve singing and improvising, outside on a lawn, or even in the sea, playing his composition "Watermusic" by drumming on the water. Around that time, some people asked John for saxophone lessons and he started teaching individual lessons.

John also wanted to create a music ensemble again, this time for children playing 'real' instruments -- not only small percussion, but also flute, guitar, and so on. He put an advertisement in the village newspaper and soon got a small group together that rehearsed every Saturday. John was paid for it by the city. Several of these children, including Peter Ole Jørgensen, Thorsten Høeg and Katrine Suwalski, went on to become professional musicians.

John teaching music at an elementary school in
North-Sjælland, Denmark, ±1974

Thorsten Høeg remembered noticing "this tall, black, stately man walking around in our suburb, which was very unusual in the '70s. Then I heard he was a musician, and that he also had a very strange, young improvising band. In the same period I was working at the music library and I recognized him on the cover of the New York Contemporary Five record. I was flabbergasted. One day at work, he stepped in and in English I asked him: 'Can you teach me to play the saxophone?' And he answered me in Danish, 'Ja, men har du en saxofon?', even with a little Jutlandish accent. 'Do you have a saxophone?' 'Nej.' No.

"One week later he came back to the library with an alto saxophone. He said he got it for me from the widow of an old musician, and he gave it to me. I still play that vintage Buescher. Then he taught me to play in a both technical and spiritual way, mostly both to be and to play yourself. He also taught me to read and write music. After a year I became a member of this improvising band: The John Tchicai & Festival band. We learned all kinds of things. For instance, at that time, John could step on magazine pictures of politicians, and that meant, if he stepped on him, a right-wing politician, then you had to play like this. And if he stepped on this one, then you had to play another kind of thing, and then he had colors and numbers that meant maybe more beautiful music, or more meditative music, but every time he stepped on the politicians, we had to do something very different. That was extremely good, we learned a lot about how to be both free-minded and very disciplined."

The saxophonist Katrine Suwalski was about 10 years old when she joined John's children's group with her elder brother, bringing a flute with her. "I was trying to fit into that group and I remember John said to me: 'Play long, low notes.' We practised that and it was actually impossible because my flute was so old and dry, you couldn't play a low note but I was trying. And then I could also play a little bit of piano, just a little bit, and I did that, and he said, 'Keep going,' and then I had to keep going for, you know, half an hour, and all the others were making wild sounds around me and moving around me, and I was like, 'What's going on?'"

John sold the big Volvo to buy a small Fiat. Since he was always driving alone in it, he found a big boulder and put it in the passenger seat to keep the car in balance. He considered himself a hermit.

Katrine Suwalski remembered how she and her brother often went to eat with John after rehearsals. "He lived in Rungsted in an old white house, on the upper floor. In one end of his living room he had this very special place behind a screen where he did his meditation. He was very much into meditation at that time, and on the wall he had a photo of an Indian guru, always in a warm spotlight. John said, 'I never switch off that light at night time.' We said. 'Ooooh...' 'And he has a very long name, this guy here' (his guru Narayanananda).

"It was at the same time cozy, exciting and mysterious. You could feel that John had a special energy, but he was not difficult to talk with or anything. You were never scared of John. He was just totally open and down to earth, a very natural person to be with. He'd always be curious -- 'Who are you, and what do you have to say? What do you have to say on your instrument?' -- and he always listened very carefully."

John stuck with his meditation and yoga practice all his life. In the '90s he added pranayama exercises, centered around the breath, to his routine. He never stopped doing hatha yoga and only slowed down a little when he became older. He watched what he ate, didn't drink much alcohol and didn't smoke.

John was a workaholic. I remember him saying: "Work needs to be done. Are you afraid to work??"

He became a spiritual activist: a serious activist for love and understanding, to be reached in a joyful, happy and often funny way throughout his career, using his music. In 1975, he wrote in a page-long newspaper article that since we're all one on this planet and in this cosmos, we should help each other to be happy and to live our lives to the full potential, "in order to reach the Divine in ourselves".

With his spiritual training, John was better able to navigate his mind and actions and to become calmer and more relaxed, with emotions under control.

John found spiritual work very important for a creative training. "For creative work you need a certain freedom to search for new possibilities and experiment with the unknown and the uncertain. You need to be confident and courageous enough to try out an idea by playing it," he said, "even if you don't know whether it will sound good or bad.

So as an improvising musician you should really be in touch with the moment. By listening, looking and feeling what's going on around you, you can feel which notes need to be played. You need to use your intuition, almost let the notes play themselves and not allow your thoughts or emotions to stand in the way." The music shouldn't be about you but about the music itself. "One should keep the ego out of the music," John used to say.

In a way, John was talking about mindfulness. Although this word wasn't much used in his days, John's work is all about embracing the present moment for the wonderful moment it is, and learning "to allow the Spirit and the creative forces of the moment to work out the music for you. Improvising is like breathing. When you breathe freely, you are in tune with yourself, and everything requires less effort."
He once wrote a composition called 'Yogi in Disguise' and explained he himself was that yogi, disguised as a musician.

Meditating with John

When I moved in with John and witnessed him meditating daily, I saw how concentrated it made him and I wanted to learn this practise of concentrating the mind as well.

John told me to use a mantra as a help. A mantra is a certain phrase that you keep repeating in your mind. John used a mantra that his guru had given to him which was a series of Sanskrit words. But a mantra doesn't have to be Sanskrit; you can create your own series of words as long as you use it correctly.

In the beginning, it's hard to make your mind stay with the mantra. Instead, your thoughts wander off and go all over the place, from your breath to the kitchen sink to your friends, your job, and suddenly you find yourself on an island in the sea or anywhere else. When you notice your thoughts have wandered off, the skill is to not fight them, but to observe and acknowledge your thoughts and then, rigorously, take them back to the mantra, back to the here and now, where once again you try to keep them.

If you train this regularly, it will become easier to control your thoughts and be focused. Your mind will be sharpened and this effect will carry over into your daily life, where it will become easier to concentrate. And if, in daily life, you notice your mind is getting distracted, you can call up the mantra at any time and recite it a few times in your mind, to recenter your concentration on the matter at hand.

This is how John told me he started his meditation discipline and it is also how I started mine. Later, John didn't need to use his mantra anymore to get into a state of meditation. Then he also used other techniques. I think he had several.

5

EXPANDING, ENLARGING

By the mid 1970s, John's spiritual practice had become the center of his life and philosophy and he lived alone in a small rented apartment in North-Sjælland. He didn't perform in public until 1975. Then it started up again.

It began with an invitation to come play with the Swiss pianist Irene Schweizer, the South African drummer Makaya Ntshoko and the German bassist Buschi Niebergall at the Willisau Festival in Switzerland. John played alto and soprano saxophone, and even some piano by playing an ostinato figure on the bass end of the keyboard while Irene improvised using the rest of it. The concert became a very lively and inspiring free improvisation. "Playing with John was always fun," Irene said. "You never knew where he wanted to go or what he wanted to do but it was always fun."

The set was recorded and came out a year later as an album titled *Willie the Pig*. It was John's first release after five years of introspection and on this record you can hear how his mind training had influenced his music. In his playing you can almost hear him meditate. He plays a couple of notes and repeats them in different ways, by changing the timbre or dynamics, or by changing a few notes... Little by little he tells a story, and he does it so consciously and deliberately that, as a listener, you can follow the journey that he improvises. While the other musicians are improvising freely and go all over the place, John's structured playing anchors it down.

Charlie Kohlhase remembers how, on his return to action, John's playing showed an increased interest in the rigorous development of motifs. "That was the thing that really moved me. That's the period of his playing that struck me a lot. What I really think about John is rhythmic precision. He had very remarkable time, and he had this way of displacing the rhythm and still landing on his feet, that's very rare. That's a thing that really impressed me about him.

"What you call ostinato is, I guess in some cases, is the way John would develop a phrase. He would like, just play a phrase, then repeat it, and build on it. That's something I try to emulate from him. He was very brilliant that way. A writer somewhere said, the way he'd present stuff like that is considered to be like a composer, really working out phrases. He wasn't just blowing a bunch of stuff."

In a way, playing ostinatos in the music, as John did, is a bit like meditating on a mantra. You keep repeating the melodic-rhythmical phrase and try to put new life into it every time you play it, so that you're not in a mechanical thing, but you try to say something fresh in every repetition. It helps you to stay in the moment.

You could also say that by creating ostinatos John united his two parental influences: his mother singing Danish folk melodies and his father dancing in an African, rhythmic way.

At Willisau John met old acquaintances and made new connections. There were invitations and plans for new music. From then on, John began to perform more and more, in different formats or groups. A year later, he stopped his school teaching job. He returned to full-time playing and never left it again. It would be impossible to describe everything he did and everybody he played with, so what follows are highlights.

While teaching a workshop at Vallekilde Højskolen, John was approached by the Strange Brothers, a trio of drummer Ole Rømer, bassist Peter Danstrup and saxophonist Simon Spang-Hanssen who inspired him so much that he decided to form a band with them.

John Tchicai and Irene Schweizer. Willisau, 1975
©Gérard Rouy

John in Antwerpen, Belgium. 1976
©Gérard Rouy

In Berlin with Evan Parker, Willem Breuker and Steve Lacy,
1978
©Gérard Rouy

The Strange Brothers had been on their way home from winning a competition in France when Peter Danstrup heard the other two say that their next step should be to play with John Tchicai. "I didn't know who John Tchicai was. Maybe I'd heard the name, but they were familiar with him. They said, 'He's world-famous, so if we play with him, it will be very fine.' I thought, why on earth should he be interested in that? At that time, I think John had come out of some kind of isolation. He was very strange to me. Very nice and kind, and also kind of frightening when you saw him. He was so tall and very unusual and he was very aware of dirt and stuff. Every time he sat down, he would dust off the chair before sitting down, or if he was driving a car, he would wipe the steering wheel. He was afraid of getting dirty I think. I think he felt as if he was very pure.

"At that time it was really strange because you thought, well, he might think that I am dirty, too. I came from a very radical, political teacher-training college, and people who acted like he did, I would consider them to be crazy, more or less. So it was a big thing for me to

John Tchicai & Strange Brothers: John, Ole Rømer, Simon
Spang-Hanssen and Peter Danstrup. 1978
Photo Peter Schandorf

act together with him. But from the very beginning when we started to play, he was extremely powerful, extremely inspiring. I actually never met anybody who could inspire me that much and encourage me. He encouraged us all the time from the very beginning: 'Write some tunes, bring some tunes, what do you want to play?' He would gladly play whatever we came with, and then he would do it his way and inspire, and it was really fantastic.

"I think one of the best things you can say about him is that he was a really good inspirer, a really good pedagogue, teacher, guru-kind of person. Not in a way like, 'Do like me and you'll be home free' but 'Do what YOU want to do and we'll find out something together,' and that was really fantastic. Suddenly we were playing a lot of things, and Simon, Ole and me started to compose, we started to be creative in a way we'd never been before. Then we played a lot of gigs, we went abroad, we made a record and a lot of things happened in one or two years. Suddenly everything was up and ringing and we were traveling around and he was here, he was very strange. "

The group John Tchicai & Strange Brothers soon made a record called *Darktown Highlights*, which sounds very different from John's earlier records. The compositions, written by all the band members, have tight structures and a variety in themes and rhythms and once the written part is played, the improvisation goes in all directions. The four compositions by John are varied among one another as well: one is a jazzy theme with walking bass and drums playing swing; one is a modified Danish children song arranged on a groovy bassline; two others are typical John themes of short melodic motifs being repeated, modified and connected.

The band performed regularly in Denmark and in other countries. John was the leader and organizer. He did the bookings and all the business parts of it. The Strange Brothers were good players willing to execute John's ideas, even though they often didn't know what he was going to do next. Once they took part in a showcase organized by a Danish jazz organisation, where several top Danish bands got the opportunity to play three nights in a row in three different towns, one band after the other. Peter remembered that the group had rehearsed its programme -- but when all was set to go, just before the gig started, John said they shouldn't play what they had rehearsed. Instead they should turn the whole set into a free improvisation.

"John said, 'The moment you start playing something you played the night before, I will stop you. It's not allowed.' The first night, it didn't go so well, I felt a little embarrassed because everybody else was prepared and I had this in my head: 'I must not repeat myself, it has to be new all the time.' Then it changed. The next day we were really successful and the other groups suddenly sounded ridiculous. And the next evening they tried to put in some free (playing) and we were kind of all over the place. The last concert, I think it was in Copenhagen, we were by far the most interesting band and the other groups were like 'maybe we should try to improvise some...'

"John was really good at seeing the situation and getting something new out of it. Sometimes it seemed as if he was just going by intuition or by faith, but I think he was really thinking about things. Meditating -- 'if I do this, they'll do that; if they do this, I'll do that' -- and this contrary thing I think was a result of that. He felt that when things are in a groove, it's going to be a certain way, then he would jump off the groove and run in the other direction. Sometimes it would be a terrible idea, sometimes it would be very good, but you could never know."

John and the Strange Brothers sometimes performed in churches. Once John was interviewed by a journalist who was sceptical about a jazz group playing a programme with ten gospel songs in a church. Peter recalled his reply: "John said, 'I don't know about you, but I dedicate my work to God every day.' I didn't know that, he had never said that to me. 'So, that means…?' 'Yes, it means this is actually something I thought about and it's important to me.' This kind of music as a religious thing was something that was also a part of John. He had a certain kind of seriousness about himself and his music that I never quite understood. But it was there, it was part of his image and part of his extreme power I think, that he was very sure about what he was doing. I've never seen him hesitate, never seen him be in doubt of anything. Maybe he has been in doubt but he didn't show it to anybody. I think he was fearless, going for what he wanted to be. And that's something I think everybody can learn from."

Also in 1976, when teaching at Vallekilde, John met guitarist Pierre Dørge again. Pierre is probably the musician John has played with the most throughout his career and whose compositions and records are most present among the material John left after his death. "In '76, I decided to go to the yearly Summer Jazz Camp at Vallekilde Højskole," he said. "One week of rehearsing, playing, improvising, maybe themes, and ending with a final concert. And it was fantastic to discover playing with John and playing his music again."

A few months later, John asked Pierre if he wanted to record a trio disc with the Danish bassist Niels-Henning Orsted-Pedersen and himself. This became the LP *Real Tchicai*, which has a very intimate atmosphere as the players tackle several compositions by John, two pieces by Dørge and the Monk standard "Monk's Mood". It was issued on the Danish Steeple Chase label, whose good distribution – including in the US – led to favorable reviews. John and Pierre never performed with Niels-Henning again, but together, the two of them did, in different formats. They recorded a live duo album, *Ball at Louisiana*, during a performance at the Louisiana modern art museum on the Danish coast in a hall with sea view, where they made music that sounded very relaxed and joyful.

"What I discovered with John, especially in those years, was this kind of almost telepathic awareness," Pierre said. "When I played with John, we were so close in improvising that we could suddenly improvise a two-part voice in triads or whatever, and wait, and then suddenly get in at the same time. It was a fantastic feeling, and that feeling stayed all the times I played with John. I've never, in the musical world and improvising world, been so close to a person as to John. I never felt the same awareness, a telepathic awareness."

Outside the intimate musical conversation, however, Pierre said that he found communication with John difficult. "He was like… untouchable or something. I couldn't just speak freely with him like I could with my other friends."

Although John didn't teach schoolchildren any more since restarting his performing career, he continued giving tuition to adults, using some of the methods he had developed with the kids: he stimulated the students to create rhythms and ostinatos, to improvise, and to be playful.

As a patient, practical person he didn't spend much time talking. He just took his instrument and demonstrated musically what he meant and where he wanted to go. Through his music, the students understood what to do and that often got the message across faster and more clearly than words would have done. It was inspirational, for several reasons. First of all, you stay close to the source of the music. Secondly, hearing a good musician play an example can motivate to practise. The student may think, if I try hard enough, maybe I can play like that one day.

John invited his students to create, then he listened to what they came up with and played with that, showing how it could sound by giving it different treatments. This helped the student develop confidence and learn that even a tiny, small element can lead to interesting music. It inspired them to go on and try new things themselves.

Participating in these workshops was a way for many people to learn about John's way of creating and improvising. He was a pioneer in teaching improvisation and many of his ex-students say John helped them find their own voice. One of them was the pianist Irene Becker, who became Pierre Dørge's wife.

"John started a kind of pedagogic tradition, a style of teaching by building music up by ostinatos, making colors or giving directions in the music using signs and special scores," Irene said. "Actually I have been doing that too, as has Pierre, who got inspiration from John. Pierre called his style 'Open Door', which is in the same family. I have also been teaching in that kind of 'system', you can call it, which is a fantastic way of making people listen and concentrate on the material they have, on what they can do with it and then develop it, instead of trying to copy or spending a lot of time trying to play something that you cannot really play."

Since composition and improvisation are two sides of the same thing – creation -- it helps your improvisation skills if you also compose and vice versa. You create structure. John always encouraged his students to compose music.

"We were a big group at this Vallekilde Højskole workshop," Irene said. "We had two piano players, and everybody got a little assignment. He gave one to me and the other piano player. We should go into another room and develop a theme for the whole band with only five notes, or maybe six notes – 'these six notes, here.' Then we went into a room, and we got a beautiful composition out of that. That was the first time I learned this way of how to make structures in music and how to set limits, how to give yourself good limits to develop things in a good way. So inspiring."

One of John's standard exercises was called "Follow the leader". This ear-training exercise or game usually was a fun thing to do. It had a quick alternation between John playing a certain motif and the students playing their imitation of it. He'd repeat the motif until most of the group could follow and then he'd start making variations on it by playing with the basic elements of music: changing the rhythm of the motif; repeating certain notes; playing the motif louder, playing it softer; playing it faster; changing the pitch of one of the notes in the motif... Little by little, the music of Leader and Followers changed and while the followers were imitating what John was playing or singing, he led them through a whole improvisation. It helped develop a quicker connection between the ears (your 'inner ear') and the instrument, because the exercise had a quick pace. There was no time for the brain to get lost in thinking. If you had played a wrong note, there was no chance to re-play the motif, because your turn was over; it was John's turn to play already. But his repetition of the same motif gave you another chance to listen to it before you re-tried, which was the goal of the exercise. If John had a group with beginners, he kept the phrases simple and used maybe only three different notes, then made many rhythmic variations with them.

Then, one day at Vallekilde, John met Kirsten Iversen, who was studying to become a high school music teacher. John fell in love. Soon, Kirsten moved in with him. They married when Kirsten became pregnant, and in 1979, John became father to a daughter named Nanna. Three years later her little sister Julie was born.

John travelled abroad to play with people who organized concerts in their own country. Sometimes it was for just one concert, sometimes

Saxophone quartet with Philippe Maté, André Goudbeek and
François Jeanneau. Amphitheatre of Nîmes, France, 1979
©Armand Meignan

it led to a regular thing. He started playing with saxophonist André Goudbeek in Belgium. They made a duo record together and in 1979 they formed a quartet with French saxophonists François Jeanneau and Philippe Maté. While playing with this quartet he met organizer Gérard Terronès, who organized jazz concerts and ran a small label. He booked more concerts with them throughout France.

François Jeanneau encountered John for the first time at a concert in Rome organised by the European Radio Union. "John was the representative of Denmark, and I was the representative of France. A few years later, in '79, we founded this saxophone quartet and we played in several towns in France, Belgium and England. I used to pick him up at the airport and bring him home. He stayed at my house, and then we did the concerts. It was very nice. It didn't last long, that's true, maybe only two years. We all had so many other things to do, but it was great.

"I loved playing with John. First of all I really liked him as a person and I loved his music and the music we played. We got along as people, in music and in humor. I remember his sense of humor at a concert in England where in the middle of a piece everybody got mixed up. The piece almost stopped because everybody was making mistakes. And John had this nice observation. He said to the public, 'Don't worry, we have full control!' -- and we started the composition all over again, from the beginning. I loved it. 'We have full control.' And we were totally off. He had this side of surprises in himself and in the music he wrote. I loved it and I loved his sound."

When John had a concert coming up, he did a lot of preparation. He selected the compositions, made photocopies of the individual parts and sent the charts to the various musicians so they could practise them before the rehearsals and concerts. He also practised other musicians' compositions if they sent him their charts before the concerts.

Photocopiers existed since the late '70s but the copies were a bit expensive in Denmark and, also to avoid having to turn pages in the middle of a piece, John tried to use as few sheets of paper as possible. Sometimes those sheets were filled with scribbled notes and lines.

The drummer Makaya Ntshoko remembered the special qualities of his music: "It could be very different from one moment to the next. Sometimes it was difficult. I remember once he sent me some charts in the mail. I didn't understand where to start reading! I called him up for an explanation. And John said, 'How nice of you to call me!' as if he was pleased to be called and asked questions about the score. Why did he write charts like that, the whole paper filled with so many notes? I always thought he just tried to look smart! But his music was very original, very alive and he had such a beautiful sound in his horn. John had a lot of humor. Crazy!"

At a rehearsal John would want the musicians to get a feel for each other and they should know their parts. Then he didn't want to rehearse much more than that. He counted on the sensitivity of the musicians and hoped that at the gig itself they would have a clear mind and ear so they could listen and feel and decide for themselves when to vary the dynamics, for instance, without John telling them. He was afraid that if he tired them out at the rehearsal, they'd be less spontaneous during the concert.

The South African bassist Johnny Dyani, whom John had met in '65, was now living in Denmark in exile from apartheid. They started playing together and John became a member of Dyani's group, Witchdoctor's Son. Dyani's music was very vibrant. John remembered it giving a feeling of smoothness, strength "and something else that might be called soul-afro-love. It was very educational for me to play with Johnny, because in order to remember his compositions I had to write them down, which some-

Johnny Dyani

times took a lot of patience because Johnny very often composed on the spot and kept changing the material around. This material came in very handy later. The music was almost always great - I'll never forget the ecstatic feelings that could happen between us with Johnny laying down the groove or playing his bouncing, vital walking bass-lines."

Johnny Dyani was active in the anti-apartheid movement. He played in concerts to raise awareness. In Germany a concert series called Jazz Against Apartheid was organized in 1987 and John took part in it. Unfortunately Dyani fell sick at the beginning of the series and didn't recover. He died aged 40, far too young.

Later that year John dedicated his next LP, *Put up the Fight*, to Johnny. He often played Dyani's compositions in concerts and at workshops, and he wrote a poem for Dyani which he recited on the 1991 album *Satisfaction*, accompanied by the Polish bassist Vitold Rek:

> **The bass is the base**
> dedicated to Johnny Dyani
>
> The bass is the base - or is it the ear?
> The bass is the base, or is it the center of the face?
> Either the ear or the mind has to decide
> Slow is low, and low is slow
> Rose, arise from your bed of green strings
> and let your red colors work as a background
> for our upward moving higher pitches
> The bass is the base

In the back of his 1980 diary, John wrote: "Crossed the border 18x, record year for travelling". In later years he probably surpassed that number. John was playing so often and with so many different people in different countries that Kirsten describes seeing him stand in the doorway with his saxophone and his suitcase packed, saying, "Hi, I have to go to Germany (or Switzerland, or Portugal, or France) for a few days. I'll be back on Tuesday."

He came and went. And as it so happens, with all the traveling and all the different people he met, John also met other women who were very kind and gentle. It led to a divorce between him and Kirsten and consequently it became harder for him to watch Nanna and Julie grow up from up close. Whenever possible, John spent time with them and sometimes he brought them along to concerts or workshops. Kirsten and he always maintained a good contact.

John's travels took him to many corners of the world. It was always work-related travel, but if possible, he built in enough time to also enjoy and discover the country he was in. In 1977 he went to Iran, Afghanistan and India on his first long, two-months trip. The German multi-instrumentalist Hartmut Geerken, director of the Goethe Institut in Afghanistan, invited him for concerts and recordings in Kabul. They also played together and recorded, which led to several LPs issued over the years. This was before the Russian invasion in a relatively peaceful time for the country. Hartmut invited John to stay at his home and showed him around. John said it was a beautiful country.

On his way over, John made a stop-over in Teheran, Iran and played a concert there, and he travelled on to Bombay, India where he played at the Jazz India festival. He played in Bombay again at another festival, Jazz Yatra, a year later.

His first trip back to the US since the mid-'60s was in late 1979 when he played a solo concert in a loft in New York as part of a small series called "Soundscapes". In early '81 he played two more concerts there, one in duo with Milford Graves and one in duo with André Goudbeek.

The next long trip was to Japan in '83. His girlfriend at the time, painter Conni Maria Johnsen, had a three-month stay in Osaka, Japan, and John joined her there for two months. He worked on compositions, taught a workshop and played a few concerts in Osaka and Tokyo with a trio of Japanese musicians. The composition "Mushi Miyake" stems from that period.

Workshop in Zabo, Japan. 1983

In 1985 Hartmut Geerken, who was now stationed in Sierra Leone in Africa, invited John again, this time to come do a tour with American drummer Famoudou Don Moye and himself. On what was John's first trip to Africa, they played in Sierra Leone (in its capital, Freetown, and in the town Bo), as well as in Liberia (Monrovia) and Guinea-Conakry (Kamsar, Sangaredi and Boké).

Moye says that John was still very serious about his spiritual practice. He got up early to do yoga and meditation for a few hours and during the day he went into town to talk, hang out or play with local musicians.

He rehearsed with the others and then went to bed early. At the concerts the trio were joined by local musicians, and there were good audiences. It was a cultural discovery for both sides. One day, a good crowd had sat down on the benches in the outdoor venue to watch the concert. The trio had decided to begin the program from back stage, playing music on conch shells while standing behind the curtains. But when they came on stage, they found that the whole audience had disappeared. Apparently, conch shells playing was associated with a spiritual society that people weren't supposed to listen to or look at. As soon as the people heard the sounds, they quickly left and took their children with them.

John liked this Africa trip so much that he went back to Sierra Leone by himself in 1988. For a month he stayed in Bo. He brought a small keyboard with him because he wanted to compose a work for six players of percussion, marimba, xylophone and vibraphone. This became "Boké".

Levitating in Antwerp. Belgium, 1981
©Gérard Rouy

John worked in the mornings and in the afternoons he relaxed. He said the children of the village were very interested in his keyboard and loved playing on it. He left it with them when he went home.

At the beginning of his career John had been very serious on stage and very much focused on his music. By the late '70s, he began communicating more actively with the audience during concerts. He began creating music with them, getting them involved through singing or hand-clapping games. He used "Follow the leader" to get the people to play along. They sang a melody or clapped rhythms that he then improvised on. On an album called *Live in Athens*, recorded during a solo concert in 1980, he sings, shouts, laughs and plays with the audience. It ends with loud and long applause and John saying: "OK, the singing lesson is over!" For John this audience participation was a way of "strengthening the oneness of all beings" through music.

In 1980, John's long-time partner Pierre Dørge had founded his own 10-piece ensemble called the New Jungle Orchestra (NJO). John was a part of it for several years. The two of them played together in various of each other's projects. Pierre asked John to play on a record date for quartet (*Ballad Round the Left Corner*) and John asked Pierre for concerts, too. They both played in Johnny Dyani's group. Usually their communication went well but sometimes problems came up. In 1986 the NJO had just put out a new record that had received a five-star review in *Down Beat* and a lot of good press. NJO had been named European Act of the Year and the group went on its first tour to the US and Canada.

"That was John's first appearance in New York since the '60s," Pierre remembered, "so the audience was also coming to listen to John, and it was... you could get very spoiled from all these things, you know."

The next concert was at the Chicago Jazz Festival, a big festival at the side of Lake Michigan. "Before us were Benny Golson and Art Farmer and after us was Sarah Vaughan, and at eight o'clock on Saturday night the NJO was on. Half an hour before our show, John said: 'I don't want to play with the band if you don't play one of my songs.'

"I think it's a very telling story for John, because he would always put things in a magical, or ragged way, in another way, you know. He wouldn't directly say, 'Play one of my songs,' which he could have said one week before, but it was like... He sometimes wanted to provoke, to put some energy in the band. And that really happened. It was so tense, many of the musicians were a little angry: 'This is too bad what he's doing.' But somehow it gained energy and tension and when we played his song, that we couldn't play, we played it wrong because it was very complicated. It was a song that I never heard with other groups, it was in different meters, so, a very complex song, you would have to rehearse it in order to play it unless you were a symphony musician who could just read the notes, so it was… We played it in a sober way."

The concert as a whole gained a lot of energy and it actually became a very good concert.

Another problem took place when John had a tour in Holland with a quartet in which Pierre played guitar. "In Rotterdam, in the first set I was playing some good solos and the audience was applauding very much, but they applauded not so much when John played. Somehow they were very much into what I was playing. And then in the next set, John played the themes, played solo and then there was a bass or a drum solo and then the theme again, so I didn't play any solo in the second set. He sometimes was like, what do you call it, jealous, you know? He could do it, it was his group, so… crazy things. He was very complex and

Pierre Dørge and John Tchicai. Copenhagen, 2008
©Jacob Crawfurd

The New Jungle Orchestra in 2008, featuring John Tchicai:
Gunnar Halle, Pierre Dørge, John, Jakob Mygind, Irene
Becker, Martin Andersen, Kenneth Agerholm, Thommy
Andersson, Ayi Solomon, Anders Banke, Morten Carlsen.
©Jacob Crawfurd

sometimes it was fantastic and sometimes some other sides came by and I was saying, 'No, never again, I'll never play with him again.' But John also sometimes said, 'I'll never play with the Jungle Orchestra again.'"

Another New Jungle Orchestra project was a theater show, based on Norwegian classical composer Grieg's *Peer Gynt Suite*, which required rehearsals every day for three months. John once showed me the classical ballet steps he learned there. Pierre said he was a nice and faithful participant in that project. This was in 1989. John and Pierre also made a trio album in 2003 with the New York drummer Lou Grassi called *Hope is Bright Green up North*. And in 2008 Pierre invited John to do a special programme with the NJO dedicated to his own compositions (John and I were together then, and they even played one of mine). So they found each other again.

Some one-time projects included a tour with the pianist Chris McGregor's big band Brotherhood of Breath in 1981, recorded on the album *Yes, Please*, and a tour with pianist Cecil Taylor in 1983, which led to the album *On Two Continents*. For both projects there were a few days of rehearsals followed by three or four concerts.

During the Cecil Taylor tour a point of friction came up between the two strong personalities. Cecil wanted to teach the group a composition by ear and he wrote it down not in notes but in note names, writing the letters higher or lower on the paper if the register went up or down. This took a long time and John got impatient. He took some music paper and transcribed the phrases in regular music notation, which upset Cecil – who, for some reason, didn't want his music written down that way. They rehearsed the music and played a concert. However, after one or two nights, a colleague came to tell John that Cecil thought it was better he left the tour. John didn't want to do that and decided to stay.

Chris McGregor, Peter Seconda, John at New Morning,
Génève. Switzerland, 1981
©Bibliothèque de Genève / Dany Gignoux

It provoked a degree of tension, but the music was very good. Perhaps this time it was Cecil using provocation to create intensity.

Every once in a while in the 1980s John played with Kristian Blak's group on the Faroe Islands, an island group between Scotland and Iceland that is part of Denmark. Some of their concerts were played amid the natural environment, for instance in a cave only accessible by water, with the audience listening from boats. Another group was a saxophone sextet from Holland, De Zes Winden/The Six Winds, consisting of half a dozen saxophones of different sizes, from the small sopranino to the big bass saxophone. John played tenor in that group, which performed compositions by all band members.

For a while in the early 1980s, John lived in Switzerland, at an artists' residence in a village called Boswil on the slope of the Lindenberg mountain. There he could work on compositions as well as keeping a regular job in Zürich playing in a theater programme called Merlin,

Simon Spang-Hanssen, Marilyn Mazur, Peter Danstrup, John and Ole Rømer. Copenhagen 1981
©Gorm Valentin

which ran for at least half a year. For maybe two years, Boswil was John's base from which he went to other countries to play. His composition "Calypso Boswil" stems from that period.

After that he moved back to Denmark, where he reformed the group in which he had played with the Strange Brothers, still with Peter Danstrup and Ole Rømer on bass and drums, now joined by the vibraphonist Bent Clausen and renamed the John Tchicai Quartet. The group had a different sound now, in touch with the changing sounds of the '80s when synthesizers became popular. Danstrup was playing a bass guitar connected to a synthesizer, John had switched to tenor saxophone and Bent played a regular vibraphone as well as an electric vibraphone that had its sound bars connected to microphones and synthesizer.

"I was very happy John invited me to join his new group and I started to bring my electric vibraphone," Bent Clausen said. "I brought that in because we had a powerful sound and it would be nice to have extra colors. With the electric vibraphone you could do all kinds of ring modulation and distortion and all that. So I was working with the sound, with shaping the sound of the instrument in different ways and it fitted nicely with the power of Peter's electric bass. We were a powerfully playing group around John.

"When you play an ostinato and you go for it and you play it a lot of times, magic happens. We called it 'the magic of repetition'. Because there's something that happens when you do things a lot of times. It gets into a spiritual thing I think, it changes your sense of timing.

"John had so much power in his way of doing stuff. I think he appreciated what we did because it made him feel comfortable. We played a lot of gigs, in Europe and Morocco and what have you. We played as much as an experimental group could possibly play at that point."

John never really worked with a booking agent to find concerts. For his many different projects in different countries, he did a lot of writing letters and making phone calls. He was the only one who had the overview over all projects. Some of these projects could have been put

Duo with Günter Baby Sommer. Dresden, East Germany,
1983
©Matthias Creutziger

together by promoters in specific countries, like Gérard Terronès in France or Jimmy Metag in the DDR, the old East Germany. Then John only had to turn up and play.

Playing bamboo flute

Other times John would have a connection with a musician in another country and then that musician would organize concerts. And since the concerts of improvised jazz were not very well paid, he would often stay at the house of the musician he played with, or with other friends he met over the years. I think John liked these home stays. He could do his meditation and exercises and make a cup of tea in the morning. It gave him freedom while hosted by good company.

In the DDR, there was Jimmy Metag, who organized several tours with John in the 1970s, '80s and even the '90s. It was always a hassle to go into the DDR, and afterwards John couldn't take the money he earned with him, out of the country. He had to spend it there, so he bought leather jackets, a fur coat, electronics like a slide projector. When he put out his

Conducting the audience. Dresden, East Germany, 1987
©Matthias Creutziger

book *Advice for Improvisers*, he had several of his scores transcribed by hand by people in the DDR. Those transcriptions were put in the book.

John once told me it used to be a special experience to play in the DDR. He said the audience was much more attentive and appreciative

Concert with Wolfram Dix, Christoph Winkel, Helmut Joe Sachse, Heiner Reinhard, Dietmar Diesner and John. East Germany, 1983
©Matthias Creutziger

than audiences in the West. They had no jazz station on the radio, they couldn't go to the West to hear somebody play a concert, and concerts by known jazz musicians inside the DDR were rare. So if there was any jazz music with its freedom and improvisation going on, it meant a lot.

In Denmark, although in the beginning it was hard for John to find money and opportunities, later on he often managed to get grants to cover costs. He was also a member of musicians' and composers' unions which helped fund projects, for instance in covering travel expenses. Without these grants and funds, John could never have done all he managed to do. Musicians from other parts of the world, for instance the US, would be envious of the Danish state's support for the arts.

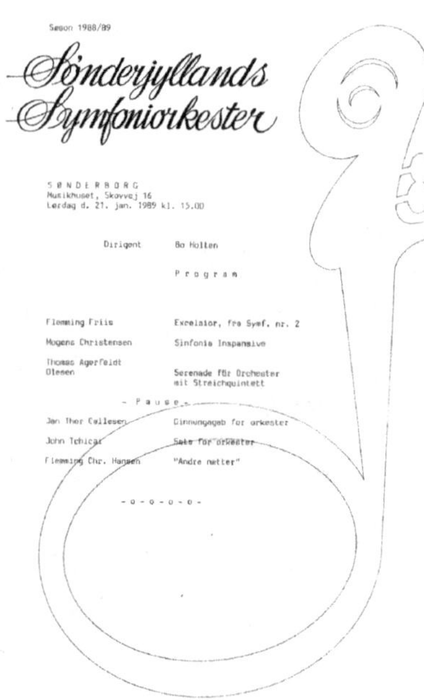

John's symphonic composition was performed in Sønderborg, Denmark, 1989

In the 1980s John made more and more compositions on commission for large ensembles. It involved many kinds of instrumentations and a combination of jazz and classical players. He wrote pieces for choir, string sections, various wind instruments and percussion. Unfortunately most of those have never been issued on disc. What's left are the scores and old cassette recordings that have been digitized.

In some of these pieces for larger ensemble John himself performed as well, sometimes with his own group, for instance in the suite for a cello trio and jazz quartet. John found three classical cello players whom he convinced and guided to do some improvisation. Together they gave a few concerts.

The music was also recorded for a film in which John recited some of his poems; the film was made but was never screened publicly.

The Esbjerg Chamber Music Ensemble put out a request for modern composers to write music for them and they performed a few of John's pieces. One of them, "Forwards and Backwards" was released on a CD titled *Anybody home?* (2003). John's dream of writing for symphony orchestra was fulfilled for a first time when the Sønderjyllands Symfoniorkester performed his "Sats for Orkester" ("Piece for Orchestra"), a six-minute composition, in Sønderborg, Denmark in January of 1989.

As his career progressed, more and more ensembles invited John to compose works for them. He declared his compositions with KODA, the Danish author's rights organization that he was a member of. KODA sent him royalties for every time his work was performed on stage or was played in broadcasts on radio or TV. These commissions and royalties formed a substantial part of John's income. Part of our house was paid with royalties earned with his composer's rights.

One special feature is Denmark's lifetime grant for artists with outstanding achievements in their field. To honour those artists and thank them for their contributions, they are paid a monthly stipend for the rest of their lives. It is awarded to a number of artists from all disciplines. In music this recognition always used to go to classical musicians and John raised questions about that. In 1990 he himself became the first jazz musician to get this lifetime grant. From then on, every month he received a basic sum which made finances a lot easier.

To make his compositions, in the 1980s John had begun using a sequencer and synthesizer. This allowed him to record one voice, and then have it play back while composing other voices to it. John had often composed music in irregular meters, and in phrases of irregular length and rhythm. Using a sequencer made this work easier. John wasn't able to print out the results from that sequencer though, so he still needed to write out the compositions in order to give scores and parts to his musicians. That transcription by hand took a lot of time and concentration.

In the early 1990s it became possible to write music using computers and when the Danish Composers' Union, which often published John's larger compositions, refused to publish his work "United Spirits of America" because it was hand-written, John started looking into getting a computer, too. From the late '90s on, John wrote the draft of his compositions by hand and I entered them into the computer which could print them out clearly and quickly. You could also transpose parts for different instruments with just a few clicks. As many composers were discovering, that saved a lot of time and made it much easier to write for large ensembles. John kept using his sequencer to find the right notes to go together until the end of his life.

John was precise and orderly. He loved paper clips to keep papers together that he put in stacks, folders and boxes. He kept three jars of pens: one in each room. When John died he left thousands of spare paper clips, pens, rubber bands and re-usable envelops.

In 1986 the Danish Ministry of Culture created a new institution in Copenhagen, called the Rhythmic Music Conservatory. John became one of the teachers and taught an improvisation ensemble class. Sometimes he also liked to present students at official concerts, to give them a chance to perform their work in public. He thought it was good for the students, but also for the public, to see a group of often young people playing very diverse and original music.

Katrine Suwalski, who as a kid had played in John's improvisation group for children was now one of those students: "When we were performing with John outside the school, he was making sure that we were all getting professionally paid for the gig. He wanted us to feel that what we did and created was valued, and that we were really doing this together. He was respecting us for whatever we could do at that time."

If students wrote compositions that he liked, John asked if he could play them in his own concerts, and he performed many pieces like that.

This made for a criss-cross of musical vibrations, taking music to parts of the planet where the student composer had never been.

Throughout the 1980s, John taught workshops in different places of the world. Many of these workshops were recurrent, like the yearly ones in Fleury in the South of France, or in Vallekilde or Holbæk in Denmark. Some workshops were set up in connection with a concert tour. If he was on tour in Holland, for instance, and there were a few days without concerts, these days would be used to offer a John Tchicai workshop.

Workshops usually ended with a performance of the work studied, and cassettes of these performances are part of John's heritage as well, whether they are in Zabo, Japan in 1983, or Mexico City in 1994. One of those was held in Alkmaar and organized by Swing, a Dutch jazz organisation. The cassette from this workshop contains a part where John answers a student's question: "How to study improvisation?" A recording of the answer can be heard on John's website. John talks about the necessity of studying and playing with rhythm, ostinatos and composition: "It's good if you can write some just simple pieces for a start, and then try them out. If you don't have a group to work with, maybe you can make a tape composition where you have different voices. Just make short pieces, it doesn't have to be any big symphony. So you make a little piece, maybe once a week, or once every fourteen days or so, and after a while you get to understand how you can work with the materials of the music. It's the same material as you use when you improvise. When you know how to work with a small theme, how to change it around and make it sound different, by doing different things to it, that's the same principle that you also use in improvisation. That's all, I think!"

Musical inspiration

John's musical inspiration came from many sources. Classical, jazz, and other music from around the world influenced his own compositions. Of the classical composers, his favorites were Bartok and the Russian 20th century composers, such as Stravinsky, Prokofiev, Shostakovitch. Their way of playing with rhythmical cells and of structuring their compositions in different sections can be seen in John's work as well. These composers influenced John's ways of connecting ideas together into a larger composition. Chopin's lyrical piano music also had a special place in John's heart. He was working on a composition based on material of a Chopin nocturne when he had the stroke at the end of his life.

Sometimes John included direct quotes of classical composers in his music as a way of weaving familiar themes into his own music. A bass motif of Mozart's "Rondo alla Turca" pops up in the middle of "Not So Black", a composition written for the Either/Orchestra in Boston with a text by poet Ted Joans. The opening motif of Bach's "Minuet in G" shows up in the end of "84 Years Orbit" on the album Life Overflowing *by the John Tchicai - Charlie Kohlhase Quintet: after a long improvisation for drums accompanied by bass and horns, it is transformed into a John Tchicai melody.*

In terms of jazz, John liked many players but he was especially a fan of saxophonists Lee Konitz and Warne Marsh. Examples of jazz standards as inspiration for John's own work are both recognisable and unrecognisable. In the ballad "Heartlights", John adapted the chord sequence of "Don't Blame Me" as the basis for a very different melody, changing the duration of each chord and the rhythmic accompaniment so that the original composition is hard to identify. On the contrary, "Aks Me Now", as the title suggests, is a very clear homage to Monk's "Ask Me Now": it be-

gins with the same motif and it follows the same chord structure as well as the same timing.

John was also very inspired by Danish folk music and used it in many different ways. The melody of lullaby "Solen er så rød mor" (on the album Grandpa's Spells) was completely played "as is" but harmonized quite differently. The ballad "Largo Lapidarius" opens and ends with the opening and ending motifs of another lullaby, "Den lille Ole", and John's lyrical melody as a whole reflects its character (on Different Places, Different Bananas and Tjak tjaka Tchicai by Pierre Dørge's New Jungle Orchestra and on Colored Air by myself).

A quite unrecognizable reworking of the lyrical "I skovens dybe, stille ro" became "I skovens dyb" (on Love is Touching by John Tchicai and the Archetypes). The original song refers to a calm, silent forest, but this version isn't calm at all. It consists of one of John's loop-creations made with a sequencer. A few ostinatos are played using the synthesizer sound "orchestra hits", and the bass notes of the original song are played in slow motion on a keyboard while guitar, bass and percussion are playing short free improvisations on top.

When John grew up, the term "world music" didn't exist yet, but the music from Africa, India or South America gave him inspiration. John liked to use drones that he found in Indian music from the late '60s on, for instance in "Orga Fleur Assam" or in his arrangement of the South American melody "Llanto del Indio". The drones and ostinatos led to a music where the harmonic color remained relatively stable. John preferred a music without many chord changes and in that sense he made no typical bebop-type jazz. He said you could do a whole lot of beautiful things without a lot of chord changes.

Music around him could also be a source of inspiration. For instance, when he moved to California he composed "Prayer for Right Guidance" (on Love is Touching). While it has a typical Tchicai style in phrases, rhythms and structure, it is also clearly a homage to Native American music.

6

WORKSHOP IN ROTTERDAM

In October of 1989, I went to a music workshop called "New Music and Improvisation" at a jazz club in Rotterdam. It lasted four evenings and had a performance on the last evening. The workshop was taught by someone called "Tchicai". Was that a Japanese name? My boyfriend, a saxophone player, quickly told me this Tchicai was Danish African and had played with John Coltrane in the '60s.

On the first evening, when I arrived at the club, a lot of people were setting up and tuning their instruments. It was noisy. I walked to the grand piano and started to warm up. Then a tall brown man with a wool cap and a tenor saxophone came to me and asked in a gentle voice: "Hi, I'm John, what's your name?"

I told him my name and then John said: "Margriet, can you play this phrase?"

He played a motif of a few notes. I listened and imitated it. "Fine. Can you keep repeating that?"

While I repeated the motif in a loop, John went on to the other people. More and more people joined in playing that same motif or something similar. After a while, all 20 of us were playing. In just a few minutes, the cacophonous noise of the beginning had changed into a much more coherent sound with a groovy rhythm. The opening motif could still be heard as well as chords and a drum rhythm. It sounded not bad at all.

Then John picked up his saxophone and played a strong, short motif which he repeated several times. People began playing that motif, too. In a question-and-answer way, John started making small changes to the motif always leaving space for us to imitate him. This lasted a while and when he stopped, John said: "OK, that was some what I call 'Follow the Leader'. Now I'm going to lead you guys by hand signs."

He explained what we were supposed to play for each different sign. For instance, a long stripe in the air meant "Play one long tone". Closing, opening and closing his hand again meant "Play one tone, change to another and come back to the first tone".

"How do you know which tone to play?"

"Use your ears. Use your sense of musicality. If you play a tone and you think it doesn't sound good with the rest of the music, then please change to another one."

There were also a circle and a square. If John pointed at you and drew a circle in the air, it meant "Create and play an ostinato". But what was an ostinato? "An ostinato is a short motif, with melody and rhythm, that you play and repeat for a long time." It could be imitated by others, or somebody could be playing chords to accompany it, and several ostinatos could be going on at the same time. A square meant you were asked to improvise freely on top of all the music going on around you.

Few words were spoken and no notes were written down, but conducted by John, about 20 people who didn't know each other beforehand were playing rhythmical, colorful music together.

After a break we continued, and now everyone got a page with regular music notes on it. It was Thelonious Monk's composition "Evidence", which has a very tricky, off-beat rhythm. The score shows almost more rest signs than notes. Playing it demands a lot of concentration and not everybody could read it. But on the other hand, it showed chord symbols, so chording instruments could provide a harmonic base for the others. It led to a more standard kind of jazz improvisation: the theme, the "melody", was played twice, followed by different choruses by individual players -- guitar, saxophone, trumpet, piano, etc. -- followed by the theme again in the end.

The reactions of the participants to this piece were varied. Some were happy because they were used to improvising on chords or because having the chart gave some security. But others weren't, because they couldn't read music or they just wanted to play free. It was clear this workshop was a meeting of people with very different musical backgrounds and levels.

Over four nights we practised a great variety of music. We played existing compositions by Monk, Ornette Coleman and Johnny Dyani in various styles and rhythms. We also did some free improvisation and we played two original Tchicai compositions with a very different structure each. His "Nutcracker" was pretty straightforward, although it went back and forth from 3/4 to 4/4. What really impressed me was his "Don't Lose Your Way" which sounded to me as if architecture was coming to life. On a big A3-sized sheet of paper there were six sections of hand-written music notes, all in different meter and not in any specific tonality. One section took care of the bass ostinato. It contained two 6/4 measures with many sixteenth notes in them, written in four voices assigned to four different players. Our bass section of two basses and two pianos practised and created a very thick bass line together. We practised the other sections, too, and were told to put marks on the score to indicate the order of the sections, because the route to take went criss-cross over the page. We played, and slowly an impressive musical construction began to take shape. This was the first time I played in such a big group and this piece especially made a big impression on me.

The last evening we performed our program for an audience of music lovers, friends and family. My boyfriend came to listen. When I asked him in the break between sets if he liked it, he was enthusiastic and said: "It's fantastic!" He was very impressed with John. "What a sound! It's so strong and beautiful! The thing he did with the Ornette melody was wonderful! And the repertoire is so interesting. John Tchicai has great taste!"

Those words made me take a closer look at John and his music. It was true his sound was very strong. He had played along with us during the theme of Ornette Coleman's "Beauty is a Rare Thing" and yes, that had been very lyrical, beautiful and expressive. But what I liked even more than his own sound on the saxophone was the way he organized the music. It had so much variety and life in it, that even though we were just a bunch of workshoppers it felt like we offered an interesting programme.

"Would you like to stay with me for a longer period?" John asked me, after a few weeks spent together, two years after the first workshop I did with him.

"Sure, it's nice."

"That's wonderful! But then I have to explain you a bit how I like to live my daily life. Because it's a little peculiar. Some women are put off by it."

"Oh? Tell me more."

"I have a daily schedule. I like to follow the rhythm of that schedule when I'm at home and also when I'm on tour. I feel it keeps me balanced. So if you don't like that schedule, we may have a problem. Here's what I do: I get up early, when the rest of the world is still quiet. Then I meditate and I do exercises. When that's over, I have a small breakfast and I do some work. And when I'm done with that, I'm ready to do other things, like, go out of the house or something."

It sounded reasonable to me. "Why do other women have a problem with that?"

"Sometimes they don't have the patience to wait for me to finish my schedule."

I understood, but saw no reason not to try.

This was the schedule he followed 350 days a year. He got up around 6 a.m. and sat down for a meditation of about an hour. Then he would make some tea and a piece of rye bread for breakfast before doing more exercises, for instance pranayama (yoga/breathing exercises). That could also take an hour. After that, he'd eat some more and tend to work. Sometimes this would be musical work, working with notes, with an instrument, a piece of paper, his keyboard or sequencer. Sometimes it would be business work, like writing letters. When he was done with that, often it was lunchtime and John liked to have a hot meal for lunch. We took turns cooking meals. In the afternoon he'd go out to get some air and do chores like going to the post office or to the copy shop to make photocopies of charts and send them to musicians he played with. Or he'd go into nature. In the evening, he went to hear music, watched a movie on television, or turned back to music to continue working. He didn't go to bed late, didn't smoke and didn't drink much alcohol.

This was John's rhythm. When he was on tour he also tried to maintain it as much as possible, at least by doing a meditation in the morning.

He was always busy, and often it was work-related, but it was always in a relaxed way. He played his musical rhythms in a relaxed way and he did the same with his life-rhythm.

It was a nice rhythm to live next to, although you really had to be calm in the morning and make no noise. It also meant it was very difficult to get him out of the house before midday, and sometimes that was a drag for me, for instance when we were traveling and I wanted us to go out in the morning. But John was a Taurus: once he set his mind to something, he did it, and you almost couldn't get him to change his mind.

As a real Taurus, you could also be sure there were regular meals or snacks, like coffee with a piece of cake in the afternoon or a meal before the concert. Sometimes it was to the frustration of fellow musicians, when in the middle of a rehearsal or a recording session, or just before the concert was going to start, John would say: "OK, now let's get something to eat." As vibraphonist Bent Clausen said: "Food went through John rapidly." John himself liked to quote what he heard (fellow Taurus) Duke Ellington say in an interview: "I like to have my main meal in the morning, because you never know when you'll get something to eat." John ate often, but he didn't eat much. His tempo was slowly but surely.

Also, when he was at home, he didn't work on music for hours at a stretch. He just worked for a little while, for instance to solve a specific problem and then he'd do something else. He said working like that kept his mind fresh. But he would get back to it soon again, and he had this rhythm every day. "Little by little, and if you stick with it you advance." That was his motto.

Composing collages

John saw himself as an improviser and a composer because he always used both elements though not always in the same degrees. I don't think he ever wrote a composition that was 100 per cent composed, meaning performed exactly as written without any improvisation in it, but he wrote many compositions that all have different degrees of improvisation in them.

John loved to improvise because it allowed him to be spontaneous and use the moment's energy for playing music that is alive. And he also loved to compose specific musical structures that anchored the music and gave it stability and strength. Structures could be given in many different ways.

His way of composing was often a matter of piecing smaller or bigger ideas and variations, melodies and ostinatos together into a larger musical structure. He added chords or created countermelodies, he wrote a melody to a bass line or the other way round. He added different sections and made transitions from one section to the next. He indicated sections where he wanted the musicians to improvise, for instance on top of a bass line, ostinatos or chords (where the bass line could be played by piano or horns, it didn't have to be the bass itself).

The improvisations could be short or long. Sometimes a free improvisation could be a way of transiting to a next section when the player, for instance, had to end his improvisation in a new key or in a new rhythm. That could make for smooth transitions between sometimes very contrasting sections. Sometimes the mood changed very much going from one section to the next, by changes in rhythm, tonality or texture. Through these changes and through all the improvisation inside and in between compositions, a listener was led through a field of changing colors. The music became a kaleidoscopic collage. As Charlie Kohlhase put it, "John's compositions could feel like three-in-one, three compositions within one."

At some point he would want to play it with other musicians and see what the different instrumental colors or textures could add to the composition, as well as what the musicians could bring in with their creative suggestions or personal qualities. Sometimes he wrote with the musicians who would perform the piece in mind, so that he could try to bring out their special individual qualities. For musicians who were great improvisers but not such good readers, he kept the writing concise and left space for them to improvise. And when playing with good readers or classically trained musicians, he could write many notes. He tried to find a way to make the musicians shine.

Often at the moment he brought a composition to a group, it wasn't completely finished. By playing it with the group in a rehearsal, seeing them and hearing them, he took final decisions about who plays which part, who starts a certain part, faster or slower, or another rhythm... A little bit like a choreographer who creates a piece largely during the rehearsals by seeing the dancers make the movements and adapting his plans when necessary.

Over the course of his career, John wrote for many different instrumentations. It could be for a standard jazz instrumentation, with at least bass and drums, or there could be other formats: a saxophone quartet or sextet; a classical cello trio combined with jazz quartet; a double quintet of horns and strings; choir and instruments...

He wrote for traditional acoustic instruments but he also moved with the times. Whenever he came across a new instrument, he was interested in its sound possibilities and he was always willing to experiment. In the '80s, when synthesizers became popular and when his co-musicians played instruments like electric bass, bass synthesizer and electric keyboards, John incorporated these sounds into his palette. He also had his own synthesizer and used sequences of different sounds as a background for melodies. He made collages of pre-recorded music combined with 'live' music, for in-

stance "Moondust" on the album Grandpa's Spells, *where Peter Danstrup improvises on double bass over a slow, calm sequence of synthesizer sounds.*

John wanted his music to be uplifting, and he worked in a playful way. His compositions have a lot of variation. Some of them have large written-out sections with intricate rhythms and harmonies, and others have just a melody, a few rhythms or an ostinato, or some enigmatic drawings or instructions. It could lead to a sometimes chaotic but joyful music. A John Tchicai composition could be a chaos with some kind of order.

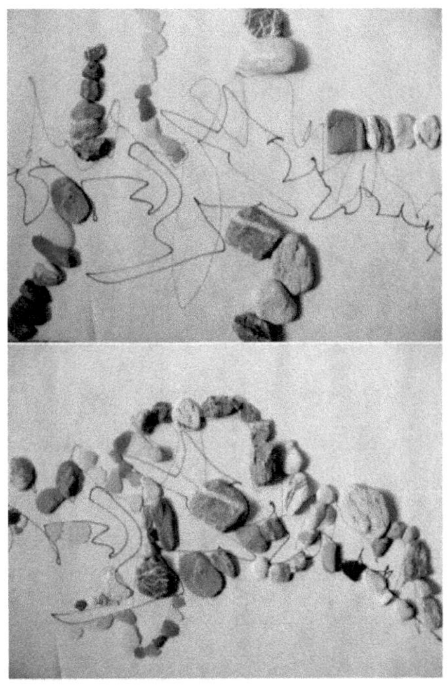

Stones on paper: sketches for a
composition? Photos by John. 2009

7

CALIFORNIA

By the late 1980s, John's ex-wife Kirsten had been a schoolteacher for over 10 years and she was looking for a change. She explored the idea of exchanging jobs for a year with a teacher in another country to get a chance of experiencing life in another culture for her and the children. The USA was an option. Kirsten asked John if he wanted to come along to help take care of Nanna and Julie, who were 12 and eight years old. John said yes. He wanted to help her and his daughters, and a nice advantage for him was, this way he could live in the USA again and see how he liked it after so many years.

He suggested she take the exchange offer from a teacher in California. A friend he had met recently, a journalist from San Francisco called Ken Bullock, had told him California was a region with great possibilities. Kirsten chose California and in '91 John went with her, Nanna and Julie to Davis, California for her exchange job. The children went to school and the plan was John would do his regular work at home and go back to Europe on tours when necessary.

However, that summer he got into a relationship with me, a piano player from Rotterdam, and he asked me if I wanted to come along. He said he'd always wanted to have a companion who shared a spiritual practice with him and who was also a musician. He said he often felt lonely when touring from one town to the next, being with different people all the time and he would love to have someone who would travel with him and be a constant factor in all of his life. I said yes.

Kirsten, Nanna and Julie were in a house on one side of Davis, and John and I moved into an apartment on the other side of town. It certainly caused problems sometimes but this is when all our lives started mingling. And in the summer of '92, when the time came for Kirsten and the girls to go back to Denmark, John and I stayed in California.

After he arrived in Davis, a small university town near Sacramento, John started checking out the local music scene, which mostly featured folk, rock, country, and some traditional jazz. Looking for people to play with, John placed an ad in the local music shop, asking for female musicians interested in playing adventurous music. No experienced musician or jazz musician replied, but a young guitarist and art student, Mark Oi, called him. He said he wasn't a woman but if possible, he liked to try out anyway. John and he got together and played. Mark came from rock and world music, couldn't read notes and had no experience playing free improvised music, but he had good ears and John was happy with him.

John explained he had added the word "female" in the ad to encourage women to feel included and react, so it could become a mixed group. He said women musicians had a different musical sensibility than men and that it was important to have that female sensibility in a group. More musicians joined. I was the only woman in what certainly was a mixed group: ages ranging from 21 to 55 (John was the only one above 30), with roots in four continents and backgrounds in free jazz, rock, classical and world music. We had two guitarists, Mark Oi and Michael Grandi, Jeff Simons on bass, Andrew Enberg on drums, Basho Fujimoto on percussion, me on keyboard and piano and John on saxophones, bass clarinet or bamboo flutes. To point up this diversity, John called our group the Archetypes.

Not afraid of going back to basics, John started to work with us by playing a few charts of himself and a few by others, and by doing basic games or exercises in improvisation. We were a sort of workshop orchestra for him and a laboratory where he could try things out. We practised every week and had an early debut concert after three months when Koncepts, a jazz organisation in Oakland, offered John a concert.

John Tchicai and the Archetypes: John Tchicai, Andrew
Enberg, Jeff Simons, Basho Fujimoto, Michael Grandi, Mark
Oi, Margriet Naber. Davis, 1993
©Russ Tucker

This was his first West Coast appearance and the reception was
mixed, with some people wondering why John played with kids who
belonged in the rehearsal space. But we kept at it. We practised twice
a week and were very inspired, creative and productive. Soon we had
30 compositions, many by John and others representing the other band

members, very diverse in atmosphere and in structure. Some were very open. Others had complicated written phrases in them that took some time to be learned by the band. A lot of them were very groovy and the grooves were sometimes unusual in 5/4 and other meters.

Since we didn't have a lot of official gigs in the beginning, we played at parties and occasions where people danced to our jazz-rock-world-free-classical music. People liked the groovy parts and the craziness, the unexpectedness of the music. Sometimes during a show we would do a vocal "Follow the Leader" with the musicians only or with the audience, or we'd all recite some lines from a poem. We did anything John asked us to do and got a bit of a following. We thought we had a great concept and were going to storm the world.

We were young but John himself really hoped to get this group through to the world and become known, maybe not so much for the economics as for making this music heard and transmit his message of love and living together in peace, harmony and creativity. We had a business card that read: "Fusion of souls with music for a better realization of the oneness of all beings". His enthusiasm was contagious.

One of John's projects was the creation of a participative slide show: it was a combination of slides and music. The images included texts to be recited by the audience, and we improvised music in reaction to the audience's sounds. It was a fun thing to do. It seemed to stimulate a feeling of community and that gave John the idea to present it at other places in California, the "freedom-loving state". John got a directory of California's 70 communities and we sent a promotional letter to each of them, without a single response. We did the slide show only one more time, a few years later.

John was less known in California than in Europe. Very few of his LPs had been released in the US, so people hadn't heard the work he'd done in the 30 years since *Ascension* with Coltrane.

Some people expected him to be still playing free improvisation with a lot of loud blowing, and they were shocked to hear us play with electronic instruments, synthesizers, groovy tunes, own compositions and a standard here and there. On the other hand, John didn't want us to play music in the way some people still thought "avant-garde" music should sound like. In situations of free playing, he instructed us: "Structure the music, play an ostinato or something. Don't play that avant-garde music of the '60s!"

We had a lot of luck in meeting people who became friends and helped us make further connections in the musical world of Northern California. John's friend Ken Bullock, a music and theater journalist from San Francisco, introduced us to everybody in his network who had something to do with promoting music, and one connection led to the other.

We also met elementary school teacher and jazz fan Russ Tucker, at whose school we played many times. Russ, an American married to a Danish woman, had been looking for John at a New Jungle Orchestra concert during the jazz festival in Copenhagen that summer. Pierre Dørge had told him: "John is gone, he moved to somewhere in the USA." Then it turned out Russ was living in the same town, two streets away from us. He invited us to perform in his classroom and later for the whole school.

On occasions like that, John led the kids in playing and singing while we played our instruments. If there were children having band-instruments with them, he involved them as well.

Russ Tucker remembered: "First they played a few pieces by themselves, and then they interacted with the kids... There was this boy in my class who had problems and was often disturbing the others. But at that moment he concentrated on his clave rhythm and was really getting into

School concert by John Tchicai & the Archetypes at an
elementary school in Vacaville, CA, 1995
©Russ Tucker

this thing. For five minutes he became important to himself and to the vibrations of the world in that room."

Russ also introduced us to his music related connections, for instance to Marta Ulvaeus, who had a radio show at the university. In turn, Marta introduced us to John Stewart, who ran the department of African American Studies where John got to teach classes, and whose poems he later recorded on *Truth lies in between*.

Of course, as in other phases of his career, John also had other projects going on during the period of the Archetypes. Sometimes he went to Europe for a tour and in one of them, John took part in the Danish Jazzpar Prize project. In '92 that annual prize had gone to saxophonist Lee Konitz, who received a money award, a record contract and a tour through Denmark with two other bands. John was asked to form one of the bands, since he had been influenced by Konitz so much. He could invite a guest and chose his old friend Dutch pianist Misha Mengelberg. John and Misha hadn't played together for 15 years.

The music for this project had a lot of variety. There were some old jazz compositions, new original compositions by John, Misha and bassist Peter Danstrup, arrangements of Danish folk melodies, and improvisations around pre-recorded music. The old jazz pieces were by Jelly Roll Morton, one of the first composers in jazz. John wanted to play his music and see how he could give it his twist. Morton's piece "Grandpa's Spells", the title track of the resulting album, has Misha improvising freely over its harmonic structure played by bass and drums.

A new musical procedure John introduced during this Jazzpar project was using pre-recorded music in the live show. With a floppy disc containing musical sequences created at home, he went to a studio in Denmark and recorded them on tape with the synthesizers available there. In the concert hall this taped music was combined with live playing. One piece started with a sequence of bell sounds to which the South African drummer Gilbert Matthews improvised. Then the pre-recorded music faded out and only Gilbert's live playing remained.

For "Heksehyl", John had written a bass ostinato in 5/4 that he asked me to write chords for, to be played by Misha. Thinking a Real Professional Musician was going to play it, I wrote chords of five different notes in a rhythm that fit the ostinato. John liked the chords but then changed the timing and he said: "I moved your pattern a few beats on in the measure, I hope you don't mind? I think it sounds nicer." Now it hooked into the bass ostinato in a different way than I had planned. It looked, and was, very complicated and Misha didn't want to play it. So Misha played a solo in this piece, and for the recording John asked me to play the chord pattern. This way I learned to not write things that were too complicated, because you might end up having to play it yourself.

When news got around that John Tchicai had moved to Davis, a lot of musicians from Sacramento and the Bay Area expressed an interest in playing with him. They organized gigs with him, or John just got together and jammed with them. The drummer Peter Apfelbaum, the multi-instrumentalist Tony Passarell, the percussionist Babatunde Lea, the bassist Bill Noertker, the saxophonist/flautist Francis Wong, the pianist Vijay Iyer and many more were among them. John's presence became an influence on the Northern California music scene.

In San Francisco's North Beach district, there was a small performance space called Bannam Place Theater. In 1993 John presented a seven-week series of Sunday-afternoon concerts there. Every week he played in the company of one Bay Area musician and one person from the Archetypes. That brought nice mixes. That's how John got in touch with the bassists Herbie Lewis and Lisle Ellis, the saxophonist Glenn Spearman, the violinist India Cooke and others. By the last week there was a long line of people waiting to get in.

Tony Passarell from Sacramento organised festivals for "adventurous jazz" that saw people like Charles Gayle, Roscoe Mitchell and the Either/Orchestra come through town. If John was home, he played with them, too. Later he and the drummer Mat Marucci began a long-time local co-operation.

Davis was only an hour's drive from San Francisco so if John had a gig in the Bay Area, we left early, took a packed lunch, went to the beach and ate it on the ocean shore, relaxed, and then went to the rehearsal and/or concert.

Throughout his career, John practised his instruments on a regular basis. He usually did this at home but sometimes he went to unusual spots. In Davis there was a period he wanted to practise and record his bamboo flute playing. This needed to be without extraneous noises. The problem was, we lived in an apartment and had neighbors downstairs and next door. So he got up early in the morning and then practised and recorded inside the walk-in closet. Nobody complained. John later dedicated one of the resulting recordings to his daughter Nanna (as 'Butterfly Going Home' on *25th Ninth World Music Release*).

For practising the saxophone, that approach didn't work. But then John found a place in the middle of a freeway intersection, with trees and a small lake. He figured out how to gain access to it and for a while he went there regularly with his saxophone to practise. He didn't disturb anybody except for a snake that seemed to come check out what was happening; it came closer every day. It checked out John's saxophone case, which John loved because he found snakes interesting. One time a cop came by, asking John what he was doing there.

"Practising my saxophone."

The cop said okay and drove off.

Whenever we could, we went on trips to discover the nature of California. It had so much beauty and variation.

The ocean, the foothills and the mountains, the large open space, creeks and rivers, the coast with the smell of eucalyptus trees, the sun and the warm air... we loved it. We asked everybody we met about nice places in nature to go to so we got to know the region quite well.

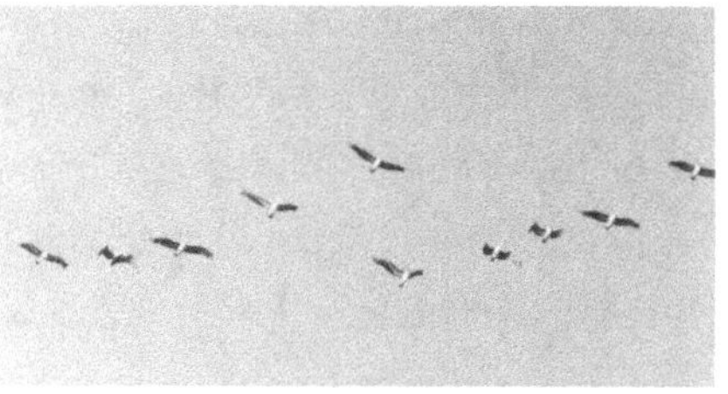

Pelicans along the coast

Diving into Yuba river, CA 1994

Nature trips like that could bring up an idea for a composition. It could come from anywhere. John whistled a lot. As soon as possible he would take a piece of paper, get his glasses and a pen, and scribble something down. At home he would start working on the idea with his saxophone, on piano or on the sequencer. His basic guidelines to help determine what to develop and what not, were: strive for beauty; use your musical sense; if it doesn't work, don't fret but move on.

John was such a passionate teacher that he sometimes even taught while he was on stage, during a concert. Then he could turn around to a musician and instruct in a clear, sometimes loud voice what this person should be doing. John could be very strong in his remarks if he thought the person was resilient enough to take it. But on stage it could be embarrassing, both for the player and for the audience. From the other hand, the musician would be learning something and the audience could hear that.

We once attended a masterclass for school children at UC Davis that was open to the public, taught by saxophonist Joshua Redman. During the question & answer session, John asked Joshua why he sounded so stale and old-fashioned. Had he perhaps never heard of free improvisation, of Ornette Coleman, Cecil Taylor, Sun Ra, John Tchicai or even his own father, Dewey Redman, who had played with Ornette Coleman? Joshua said "Eh" and "Oh", and John was removed from the hall. As he was being escorted away, he said to Joshua: "Tell your father John Tchicai says hello." And Joshua did pass that message on. Years later, Dewey Redman told the story to drummer Matt Wilson, who told it to Charlie Kohlhase. At least to my ears, Joshua's playing became more interesting after the incident...

Stressing the fact that you can only advance if you rehearse and repeat, John always tried to instil in his students the importance of practising and the discipline it required. He once joked he would start an academy called the Tchicai School of Music and Discipline.

He liked practising and doing exercises himself. He encouraged students to create their own exercises and he did that, too. If John ran into a musical problem, for instance a technical problem on one of his instruments, he created an exercise around it and tried to make that sound interesting, so it would be fun to practise. Sometimes the exercises developed into compositions. "The Secret", a Latin piece included on the album *Put up the Fight*, is an example of that.

Charlie Kohlhase discovered how that composition originated: "This concert with Johnny Dyani's Witchdoctor's Son group in the mid '80s was the first time I saw John play only tenor, and his playing was very focused. I remember they did this tune of Johnny's called 'Appear', which is in the key of E. And I remember he was playing this solo, and he was kind of playing sparely and imaginatively. Then he stopped and started singing. He did this great kind of rap that goes 'Johnny, Dyani, Mbizo, Dyani, Johnny, Dyani, Mbizo, Dyani', and built off of that ostinato. And I remember thinking wow, that's like the coolest thing I've ever heard. But I've come to find out, John hated playing in that key, it was the key of F# on his tenor. So he's having a hard time playing his solo actually, which I think is why he started singing. And then I found out later he wrote that composition 'The Secret' during that tour, which is basically an exercise in playing triads in the key of F# on the tenor. Something that he used to try and improve his playing on 'Appear', had turned into another tune."

When we had a concert, John made an effort to send mailings to friends and all his new connections, and we bought a staple gun to put up flyers on walls and notice boards. But when people saw the Archetypes listed, they didn't realise it was a group including John Tchicai. When someone pointed out that his own name wasn't in the band name, John said he didn't want that. He seemed to think people should already know it was him who led the band. I think it was also out of a modesty and shyness. He also wanted to accentuate the group effort. In the Archetypes, too, he stimulated everyone to contribute compositions, and most of us did that. Though it was clearly him who led the band and who got us concerts and contracts, he saw us as a collective. Once when he was playing with singer Ann Dyer, she announced him on stage as the person leading a band called "John Tchicai and the Archetypes". Ann did public relations for the San Francisco Jazz Festival as her day job. Her expertise in marketing convinced John to include his own name. From that moment on we were called John Tchicai and the Archetypes.

One area where John himself had a good instinct was in understanding the importance of the internet. In 1994 we met a person working with computers at the music department of UC Davis who told us about internet, websites and email, all very new subjects at the time. Right away John wanted his own website, and a few months later he had one. It only had text in black letters on a white screen as was normal back then. If you searched for websites of other jazz musicians, you couldn't find them because they didn't exist. John was one of the first artists to have one.

A year later, it became possible to include photos. So John asked me to select a bunch of band photos and photos of nature. I also selected a nice photo of him, but John didn't want to include it. He didn't want to have all that attention on himself. He understood he had to advertise, but didn't want to be at the center of it. He

©David A. Guastavino

wanted his work to get the attention, not him as a person. We compromised and said we'd send all photos to the friend who made the website and let him choose which photo to put where. Sure enough, he put John's photo at the top of the first page.

John sometimes used lofty and poetic phrases that could keep you wondering what he meant exactly. If it was concerning business, then that was difficult. Sometimes when he was booking a gig and couldn't get a great deal, he did the concert anyway to have an opportunity to perform and test out material he was working on.

Little by little, John Tchicai and the Archetypes became better known. We were invited to play at the Monterey Jazz Festival in 1994, and at the San Francisco Jazz Festival the following year. We got a record deal with B&W to make an album. It was the first time John made a CD instead of an LP and the fact you could include 72 minutes of music

> **John's liner notes for John Tchicai & the Archetypes' CD "Love is Touching":**
>
> "Welcome to you. Walk, jump or crawl into the 'Oneness of All-Pool'. In this medium of electrical and vibrational sensations where things, matter, spirit, mind and anti-matter slide in and out of each other, each and everyone, we sincerely regret not being able or sensitive enough to feel your immediate responses. It's a magical process in part only. It is our hope that someday, when we meet faces open like books and senses eager, we'll experience magic in its totality together. In the meantime enjoy the rays of organic intelligence coming to you from individuals living in Californian Culture and Global sunlight. Don't be alarmed, frightened or embarrassed by our free language. As inventors we hate conservatism and introduce new elements ad libitum into the world music language. Don't get anxious or desperate when you can't hear the difference between the conventional instruments and the pre-recorded synthetic structures, don't know whether a specific track is recorded direct to DAT-2 track, 8 or 24 track, or can't detect when we change between playing written charts and playing from graphic notation or are improvising freely. After all, at this stage, dude, the whole thing is mechanical, unless of course, you approach the piece of art with your tactile sense and your emotional gear. Approached from this angle, we can promise you a much better communion with the organicunities of this product."

was very impressive. We had many compositions and we filled the CD. The deal was good, and we were given four evenings to record.

Then something strange happened. We'd been together for a few years. Some of our pieces were 'old' by then, and John suddenly wanted to record them in a different way than we were used to playing them. It confused the band a little. Most of us had very little recording experience. As a result, the playing was less groovy and spontaneous than usual. We could play better than the CD suggested. The result of it was that when *Love is Touching* came out in 1995, the reviews were less favorable than we had hoped. Still, the tracks have a lot of variation and one of them is quite experimental: "Scientific Americans" is a collage of casual speech, synthesizer sounds and a lot of silence. Another track had two young poets, Mario Ellis Hill and Paul Calderon, who performed with the band now and then, rapping verses.

There was an offer for an Archetypes concert at the Vancouver Jazz Festival in Canada. Unfortunately, they couldn't afford to pay the trip for all band members. In the end John performed the Archetypes repertoire there with musicians present at the festival. The New York pianist Marilyn Crispell was one of them.

We also played in New York City at the Knitting Factory. John had been looking forward to presenting his new group in the city where he had spent a few important years. We were shocked to find out we were only booked into the basement's small room instead of in the big hall. But the room was full in any case.

That summer, too, we went on a European tour, mostly in the former DDR part of Germany. John's old friend Jimmy Metag organized it. I remember our sets were always longer than they were supposed to be according to the contract. We were asked to stick to the time. That was difficult for John. He was too driven to play and present the music.

In the following summer we came back for another tour. After that, we disbanded the group. Several members had moved away or had other activities going on. We didn't have the same intensity as in the beginning.

By the time the Archetypes ended, John had been acquiring more connections to established organisations and funding possibilities in California. We applied for his inclusion on the roster of artists eligible for funding by the California Arts Council, and after a long process he was accepted. That was a big help in organizing tours, for instance the one to Crescent City in the far North of California.

In '96, too, he was hired for a teaching program in Vacaville, a nearby town, funded by a California state programme called Arts in Corrections. In Vacaville there was a large state prison. Many people in the town either worked there or had family members imprisoned. John taught inmates at the prison one night a week and children at the school one morning per week. The inmates had band instruments and John played the music they wanted to play which was mostly pop and rock songs. He played along on his tenor sax and encouraged them, too, to compose music. When they wrote something John liked, he took the chart with him and played it outside of prison at other concerts, giving full credit to its composer. With a selected group of children in the school he played music on small instruments and worked on creating music and text. To recite that text in a rhythmical way, he developed the grid-notation used in "A Chaos with Some Kind of Order".

That same year the music department of the University of California in Davis asked John to join their team and teach an improvisation class. John did this for several years until we left Davis in 2001. There were instrumental players and there was a rapper/poet so the class was named the UCD Sound & Poetry Source. John performed with the students at local festivals like the Whole Earth Festival in Davis and the Sacramento Heritage Festival, with different students each year.

One of the projects John regularly went to Europe for was the Jazz against Apartheid project in Germany. In a concert tour that had originated around the South African bassist Johnny Dyani, John would play Dyani's music with old bandmates like the trumpeter Harry Beckett and the drummer Makaya Ntshoko. In 1997, the organisation Jazz in Flight asked John to invite a group to present Dyani's music in Oakland. That brought Pierre Dørge and Harry Beckett to California, along with Gilbert Matthews, since Makaya couldn't make it. A replacement for Johnny himself was harder to find. Jazz in Flight suggested asking Art Davis who had played with Coltrane and John on *Ascension* and lived in Los Angeles. That changed the music's character quite a bit.

The group rehearsed and played the concert in Oakland and did a workshop playing Dyani's music with local musicians. On the afternoons off we took a trip to the beach and relaxed. Pierre Dørge noted the change in John's personality: "In those years, I don't know how it was for others, but for me, John became more of a normal person that I could communicate with and make jokes with, have some social life with aside from the music."

Pierre Dørge, Harry Beckett and Irene Becker taking a stroll
with us at San Francisco Beach, 1997

Soon after that we went to Chicago. Through a news group on internet John had gotten in touch with a photographer and jazz lover there called Tony Getsug. Tony had a vision of making a record that teamed John up with the Pulitzer Prize-winning poet Yusef Komunyaaka. He sent him Komunyaaka's poems and John composed music to them. Then he gathered a group and together with Komunyaaka, we rehearsed, performed and recorded the collage of music and poetry. This became the album *Love Stories from the Madhouse*, named after one of the poems. It was on a new, small label which unfortunately stayed small.

In the same period we went to Boston, where the saxophonist Charlie Kohlhase had organized several concerts. Two years later this led to the recording of *Life Overflowing*, containing a composition called "Cancel Values", co-composed by John and me. John liked to write together with other musicians, discovering the fresh challenges and surprises that came from seeing how another composer would tackle a musical problem.

John in Chicago, 1997
©Don Getsug

John and I had this common dream that we should write a symphony together. We started the project in '93 but never found the time to really get into it. However, we did work together on composition a lot. Often John came with a piece of paper and some notes, asking if I could write chords to it, or a melody, or a counter-rhythm. For "Cancel Values" I wrote a rubato melody over a recording of two ostinatos of different meters played at the same time, which gave a busy background. Later John changed the background by taking those ostinatos out and adding a more meditative background.

That changed the character a lot but it was nice, too. It's the version he recorded with Charlie Kohlhase.

Another composition we co-composed was "All-embracing space" to a poem by John. The chart is included in Appendix 4.

John had performed with other artists such as poets, painters, dancers, filmmakers all through his career. Back in the '70s, with the Dutch poet Bert Schierbeek he had performed al-

The two of us in Chicago, 1997
©Don Getsug

ternating music and poems. In 2000, he accompanied Bobbie Bolden's dancers in a choreography. In 2009, he improvised while watching Peder Pedersen's abstract videos projected on three different screens. There were so many collaborations like this.

An unfulfilled dream of John's was to create an audio-visual document where he himself could create both elements. He was on his way doing that in a collaboration with the videomakers Diane Sosnoski and Hermine Holtland of Flaming Heart Productions in Berkeley in '97. John designed certain visual scenes of human movements and nature scenes, which they filmed on his directions. Then the material was edited into a collage. This was broadcast on Berkeley Community TV while our group watched it and improvised music to it, 'live' in the studio. Reflecting on this project, Diane says: "I remember his amazing talent and his kindness. It was so easy to work with him and he was so supportive of the ideas I presented to him."

In 1998 we spent five months in Europe. John was invited for a 10-day tour of Greece, followed by a long stay in Holland, where he taught weekly workshops in Amsterdam, Rotterdam and Alkmaar. Then he returned to Denmark, where he was chosen as Artist of the Month, which meant that for four weeks, John was the center of many concerts with different Danish musicians. In this time he recorded "A Chaos with Some Kind of Order" and other compositions with the group Ok Nok Kongo for the album *Moonstone Journey*. He was also able to spend time with his daughters, Nanna and Julie. This was something he tried to do whenever he was in Europe.

In Greece I had become pregnant and, back at home in Davis, our son was born on a cold and sunny winter day. John named him Yolo -- after Yolo County, where we were living. We hoped this name would always remind him of his roots to the place where he was born, although we were already feeling that Davis wasn't the place for us to grow old in.

We travelled within the US looking for somewhere we could really settle down. We went to the south-east of the US: to Atlanta, Georgia

John in front of our house. Davis, CA, 1998

and Florida, but found that we didn't really like the moister climate. We also went to Italy, to Puerto Rico and to Trinidad, and we liked that, but always when we came back to Davis, we thought we were better off there. We had a nice home and were well surrounded by friends.

The bassist Peter Danstrup remembers thinking of John as a nomad. "In the very beginning he was always traveling around, never having this place to stay. When he went to Davis, I think that was maybe the first time he stayed at the same place for a long time. (Now it) was, 'Where's John?' 'I think he's in Davis.' Before that, it was 'Where's John?' 'I don't know, he could be here or there, or maybe he's staying there but, last time he was there or...' You could never know."

During his 25 years in Europe, John hadn't crossed paths much with musicians he'd collaborated with back in his New York days in the '60s. He'd played a few times with Don Cherry and once with Milford Graves, and that was about it. Everybody had gone in different directions, and busy schedules prevented the occasional attempt. So he was

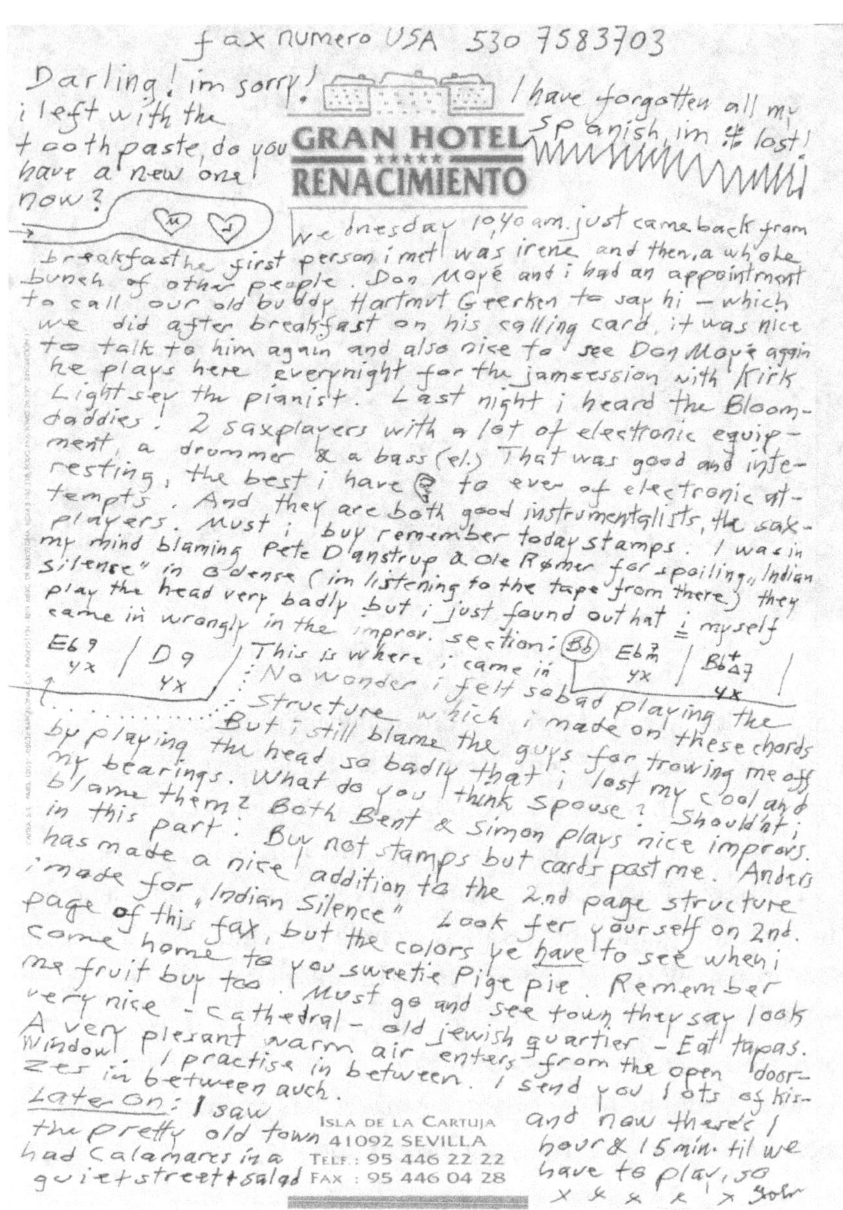

Fax from John, while on tour in Spain with New Jungle
Orchestra, 1998

happy when in 1999 the chance for a reunion concert with the New
York Art Quartet came up.

In June they played at Bell Atlantic Jazz Festival in New York as an opening set for Sonic Youth, whose guitarist, Thurston Moore, was a fan of their group. He was helpful in organizing the concert. A pre-concert dinner at the house of Roswell's friend, promoter Verna Gillis, was filmed by filmmaker Alan Roth who later published the material in his documentary about the quartet called *The Breath Courses through Us*. The music by the reunited musicians was good. They recorded an album and there were two sequel concerts in Paris in 2000 and Lisbon in 2001 but unfortunately the project had its downside.

People change in 35 years. There were different financial attitudes among the players and the communication with the promoter was difficult. In the '60s, the group was a collective and any income from concerts was always shared equally. Now, for a reunion concert John received $2,000, which was acceptable to him, but when he found out by accident in Lisbon that the total fee for the group was $20,000, he was shocked. He was so upset that he called me in the middle of the night, something he never did. He tried to discuss the problem the next day but it didn't go well. So, that concert in Portugal was the last one ever by the New York Art Quartet.

Around this time John was contacted by Kristian Høeg, a protestant priest in Denmark, who had a dream of creating a religious *Totalkomposition* with music, theatre and dance for two choirs, vocal soloists, a dancer and a jazz ensemble, and who asked John to be the musical director. It took over a year to compose the music to Kristian's libretto and it became John's largest work ever. By then fortunately, we'd had our computer music-writing program, Finale, for a while.

A large group consisting of marimbas, saxophones, bass clarinets, bass and drums in the jazz ensemble, plus classical violins, vocal soloists, a girls' choir, an adult choir and the priest himself performed John's music in three different churches in Copenhagen in May 2001. The church space was used for choreography, there were artists entering the 'stage' from the side door or the main church entrance and there were other

'Total' inventions. It lasted close to an hour and is recorded on the CD *Hymn til Sofia*.

But this musical success was overshadowed by the fact that John's daughter Nanna was seriously ill. She had been born with a muscular disease for which she had been taking daily medication ever since she was small. Unfortunately, those medicines had side-effects that were becoming worse. Nanna lost her wish to live. She attempted to take her own life and was hospitalized. In September 2001, three days after 9/11, she attempted again – and succeeded. She was 22.

John was heartbroken. For a long time he barely spoke.

The events of 9/11 meant that the airspace was closed and it was impossible to fly to and from the US. We couldn't get a flight to attend the funeral in Denmark for another 10 days, and in those tense days we decided that was it. We packed up our things and called a moving company. On September 23, we left the US and returned to Europe.

Nanna Tchikai Iversen and her dog near Lake Berryessa, CA,
1997

John's poetry

Monk's Dream

Whenever the night brings a dream along
and whether the past, present or future holds on,
all you can ever ask for is learning the dream
that takes you out of your mind.

Amorphous contraptions will give you fright,
and no explanations will set you right.
Why! couldn't you have told me before I was born,
off, you must be off.

Time flies away, what an odd day,
calm, do I wanna become calm?
Where is my island now?
With houses, grass and fields?
It could be around the corner right now.

Whenever the night brings a dream along
and whether the past, present or future holds on,
all you can ever ask for is learning the dream
that takes you out of your mind.

(music Thelonious Monk, words John Tchicai)

John was a musician who also expressed himself in art forms other than music, mostly in visual art and in poetry.

He liked visual art and he painted when he was young. Sometimes he made collages with cut-out pictures from magazines and hung them on the wall. Letters he wrote were often decorated with colors and drawings, even the envelopes could be colorful. If he was in a new city and had some spare time, he liked to visit a museum.

John was always actively making poetry. Inspiration could come from dreams he'd had, or from daily life. Often the poetry was incorporated into a musical composition. A few times he did this in a way it could be sung, like when he wrote a poem to Thelonious Monk's composition "Monk's Dream". More often he recited the text while other musicians played their instruments, as in the title track of the album Satisfaction:

SATISFACTION
to Lester Young

I want the big orgasm said the small man.
Aren't you too small for such big wishes! said the orgasm!
and the big one is difficult. You can get satisfaction,
but on the way up there's almost nothing to hold on to,
and there's lots of loose debris on these steep brown Mountainsides.
Lester said: I want a little girl! and he got several small girls
that grew older and older and then left him,
or he went off to some other place to toot,
and why stop since Lady finds nature fulfilling.
Almost never but fast like Maité.
Embrace her shoulders you who carries the crown.
Clear tones and different keys tear the paper.
The souls must be yoked at night.

Sometimes he recited the poetry freely, or he composed a rhythm for it that other band members could recite in unison. And other times he invented on the spot what he was singing, improvising from real words to made-up words and open sounds in a form of scat-poetry.

He also worked with the words of other poets. A whole album, Truth Lies in Between, *was devoted to the poetry of his Trinidadian friend John O. Stewart.*

John was also poetic in his choice of composition titles. He liked to use positive words like "love", "life", "hope" as in "Heavenly Love on a Planet", "Love is Touching", "Life Overflowing", "Hope is Bright Green up North". At one time he searched for popular songs that had the word "heart" in its title. That led to re-arrangements and performances of "In the Garden of your Heart" and "Bless your Heart".

Among his more freely composed poems is "132 Observational Measurements". The text was recited in the "Follow the leader" style: one musician recited a few words at the time, followed by the rest of the group who repeated these words exactly, interspersed with free improvisation by assigned players. Since there was so much improvisation in it, the piece never came out the same way twice.

---

132 Observational Measurements

*132 Observational measurements
combined with cosmological arguments
has done gone
1 - 2 - 7 <u>faces</u>,
3 - 2 - 1 - 8 turning upward,
27 - 38
black bones
ri-ki-ta, ri-ki-ta rattle
and caused major relationship shifts*

(_______ = loud)

8

SETTLING IN FRANCE

The summer and fall of 2001 felt as if a big whirlwind had come to California. We jumped on a flying carpet and held on to each other carefully. The wind took us around the world and all over France where, in a far corner of the south, the wind died down. We got off the carpet and started a new life.

You could put it differently and say that in Denmark we bought a car and drove down to France, stayed in rentals for a few months until we found a house. Five months later we settled into our new home.

Claira is a village in the Pyrenees, not far from Perpignan, the last big town before the border with Spain, close to the Mediterranean sea. We didn't know the area and had no idea what the tramontane was. It's a strong wind, like the mistral, that blows the clouds away. Thanks to the tramontane the sky is often blue, but it's also often very windy. If we'd known that, I don't think we'd have chosen to settle down there. But we didn't know and we stayed. Our plan to live both in France and in the USA, dividing our time between the two countries, soon turned out to be too complicated and too expensive to realize.

Once John had his studio installed in one of the rooms, he could start his musical work and pick up his daily rhythm again. He had reached retirement age now and was becoming a little slower. He no longer put up ads on notice boards in music stores looking for people to play with. He cooked for his wife and son and took Yolo to school by bike.

The task at hand

Anything can happen
from one second to the next.
Faults, blunders and accidents happen all the time
with or without our knowledge.
The task at hand is to change all ugly mistakes
into something beautiful

(music & text John Tchicai 2003, chart included in Appendix 4)

John in his home-studio, Claira, 2003

But he was glad when he could leave to go on a tour. The Roussillon is rural country that is alive mostly during the tourist season. It is relatively poor and there is very little of a modern cultural scene. In Perpignan, jazz life was hard to find. So when musicians abroad asked him to come do a concert with them, he said yes. Moving between countries had become easier now, thanks to low-cost air travel, and we lived not far away from regional airports in France and just over the border in Spain.

John was called by people he knew from before, like the pianist Kristian Blak on the Faroe Islands or the bassist Vitold Rek in Germany. He did a few more projects with Johnny Dyani's music in Germany. He also developed his connection with Charlie Kohlhase, who played in the Either/Orchestra, a big band that John had already done a concert with back in '93. Now its leader,

Russ Gershon, commissioned a special program of new Tchicai compositions, which the band performed in 2003 in Boston and New York. While there, John met the guitarist Garrison Fewell who right away asked him to do a project in Italy the next summer. From then on, John often played with Charlie and Garrison in a trio or with Garrison in a duo in Boston or in Italy. As a trio they recorded the album *Good Night Stories* and when they got a five day stay at Birdland in New York in 2007, they recorded *Tribal Ghost* in a quintet with the drummer Billy Hart and the bassist Cecil McBee.

John also made new connections. Spring Heel Jack, a duo from London, asked him to do concerts and recordings, and the journalist Barry Witherden's wish finally came true. Ten years before, he had written in the *Wire* magazine: "... Tchicai sounds like a man who feels so deeply about an issue that he quietly and doggedly puts his own point of view until those vociferous disputants with more superficial beliefs move on... he sounds like a highly individual, architectural improviser who submerges himself into the group with self-effacement... Will someone please bring John Tchicai to Britain for a tour?"

This project led to *John Tchicai with Strings*, an unusual album in which John improvised over the musical textures made by John Coxon's guitar playing and Ashley Wales's electronic sounds. The duo didn't want to play any compositions and they wanted him to play the alto, as he had done on his New York recordings, rather than the tenor he now favoured. John agreed as long as he could also recite a poem called "These Pink Roses" by Steve Dalachinsky, an American poet who had written it while listening to John in concert in New York.

Cover of John Tchicai & Spring Heel Jack's CD

Other people asked John to write a composition for them. Danish percussion/saxophone duo Duodenum performed his "Drømmerens Bevidsthed" and bass saxophonist Klaas Hekman, who John played with in the saxophone sextet the Six Winds, performed the solo composition "Four Threehorns", a four-part suite with poems to be recited as transitions between the parts. John often went to Denmark to play with drummer Kresten Osgood, for instance in a project with Oliver Lake, or with drummer Stefan Pasborg, or with the all-female Sophisticated Ladies trio … and many more.

Our son had to go to school and I stayed with him, but every summer the whole family would drive up to Denmark for the Copenhagen Jazz Festival, where John would have several concerts every day with different people who wanted to play with him.

In 2006, he was invited by someone in Israel to play a set at a summer festival in Tel Aviv that took place the day after the final concert of a tour on the Faroe Islands. John said yes, but it involved a journey with five different flights on one day: Faroe Islands to Copenhagen to Amsterdam to Paris to Budapest to Tel Aviv. After that, he complained about a pain in his leg muscles due to the many take-offs and landings. It didn't make him travel any less, though.

In Tel Aviv, John played his "Berlin Ballad", written in the 1980s in a hotel room on the top floor of a tall building in East Berlin, from where you could look out over the Wall that was still standing. The character of the piece is warm but also melancholic and a bit spooky. John explained the origins of the piece to the audience. That was his statement about the situation in Israel.

Back home in France, John composed all the time for several projects with large groups. He created a second religious work after "Hymn til Sofia". This was called "En Nutidig Pinsemesse" ("A Contemporary Pentecost Mass Composition") and it was performed in a church in Roskilde, Denmark in 2005. It became a family project, because John's daughter Julie was one of the vocal soloists and his third wife Kirsten was a singer in the choir. John conducted and played, and Yolo and I were sitting on the front row. The church was full and the Pinsemesse was repeated in a later year.

But all John's traveling took its toll on our relationship. It was hard for me to find work and musical connections in the Perpignan area, and sometimes when John came back from a tour, there was only time to say hello, do the laundry, get stuff together for the next tour and then he had to go again. That produced stress. I used to have pieces of paper on my desk with lists of phone numbers from hotels that he stayed at: 00-39-123-4432 room 203, 0049-987 6543 room 104, etc... The numbers changed every day.

For John, too, it was hard to make any musical connections in our area. It felt like a barren land. He did get a teaching job at the Casa Musicale, a cultural center in Perpignan, where for a few years he taught an improvisation class for adults, every other week if he wasn't on tour. Some musicians drove 200 km from Toulouse to attend this class.

In 2007 John did a project around Catalan folkloric music. Our area was part of French Catalogne and its folkloric music and dance, the *sardane*, is still very alive. The music is played by orchestras called *cobles* that play tra-

Gouleyrous Canyon, Tautavel, France

ditional instruments such as the oboe-like *tible*, the saxophone-like *tenora*, a three-string bass and the *flaviol*, a recorder connected to a small drum carried by hand and played with a stick. Coble Tres Vents invited

John to arrange some of his compositions for them and, since they were classically trained musicians, to guide them in any improvisation required. They were good readers but not used to improvisation. John arranged his compositions for them and after a few rehearsals they gave two performances where the special instrumental colors of this ensemble made John's compositions sound quite different.

Their flaviol player, Michel Tignères, remembered John showing them how to approach the unfamiliar demands of his pieces. "John brought some compositions with very specific structures and that got us going. He taught us to relax a bit and take some distance from the musical language which wasn't like we were used to. He taught us to look at it with respect for the written parts and respect for the indications, but to accept that it could move and change very much due to the improvisations. It was incredible. He had an extreme technique -- you could see it was someone who had a very advanced musical concept, very avant-garde. And we felt it was someone who had at the same time a foot in the tradition as well as a look towards the future. It was something at two levels at the same time. And we liked that very much. Also trying to challenge ourselves, going into the unknown, trying to find magical moments, and some moments really happened. Very interesting. And an extremely sympathetic person, very open, very accessible. John wanted to take us along and we tried to follow him."

By 2009, John and I were having too many arguments. We split up and eventually divorced but stayed in the same village. At the age of 72, he moved into an apartment two streets away. If he wasn't on tour, Yolo would spend the weekends with him. Soon, John and I became very good friends again.

John's last teaching event, a year before his death, was at a seminar of a psychologists' organisation in Vejle, Denmark. He gave a short talk and played for and with the participants. Afterwards they sent him notes, thanking him for shining light on human communication from another angle than they were used to.

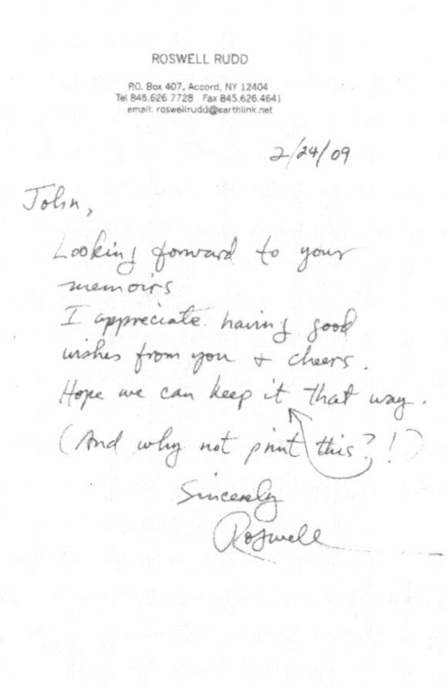

Letter from Roswell Rudd, 2009

John began to look through the archive of correspondence, photos, poems and drawings that he'd kept throughout his life and made a selection of them for a book he wanted to publish. He didn't get time to finish that.

In February of 2012, John toured in Jutland, the western part of Denmark. Always when he had to go there in the winter he got sick, and that happened again this year. But he was more sick than usual and a visit to the doctor revealed heart problems. The doctor gave him blood thinners to avoid clotting and said he should also slow down his schedule. Of course, that was a difficult thing for John to do.

In June, on his way to the airport in Barcelona, he had a stroke. He was taken to a hospital there and then transferred to a hospital in Perpignan. When a place in a rehabilitation clinic became available, John was moved there. The first week after the stroke he was often awake and it seemed he'd recover well, but after that he was often asleep. If he was awake, his awareness was low.

This lasted until Emma Caron, a student from his Perpignan class, came to visit him. She brought her flute with her to the clinic and, standing next to John's bed, she played an improvisation for him. John opened his eyes and listened to her with a smile on his face. Hearing the music, nurses came to the room and they were amazed to see John suddenly so awake. From then on, when I visited him we could really talk and communicate.

In the clinic John was given physiotherapy and he wanted to get better. When I was there we did exercises and John fell back on his old sense of discipline. One day we looked at photos of John's daughter Julie, who had come to Claira but had had to go back to Denmark. John used his glasses and after looking at the photos it was time to take them off. He wanted to do that by himself. I suggested he'd use his right hand, since the left side of his body was almost completely paralyzed. But John, who was left-handed, said: "Let's do this the way it is supposed to be done. So, I hold the case in this hand (his right hand), and then we go…"

He began the movement of bringing his left hand towards his head. The first centimetres went well, then he became slower. I supported his arm. By the time his forearm was in a right angle up, he stopped. I waited. When John didn't continue moving, I tried to bring his hand all the way to his ears so he'd have the sensation of taking the glasses off, but it wasn't easy to move his hand all the way up and it was me who took the glasses off. Then we slowly brought the arm down.

"It's funny," John said.

"What's funny?"

"While I do that movement it's as if all of a sudden I dream, and then later I wake up again."

"I couldn't see you were dreaming. You stopped the movement but had your eyes open. Are you dreaming now?"

"No."

After that, John was very tired.

In general, after the stroke John seemed quite peaceful and relaxed. In a way, he looked more gentle than I'd ever seen him in the past. One morning I arrived in the clinic when he had already been treated by the nurses and was all set for the day. After some talking he took my hand.

"You know what would be nice?" he said.

"No, what would that be?"

"If one day you can come here and then we go outside. Among the trees we can hear the birds sing."

He got a wheelchair. Four nurses had to work together to move him into it. We made trips to the recreation room, but we never made it outside.

His French improved during his stay in French care from having to talk with the French nurses and doctors. Due to being in different places and to shifts, he was treated by different people all the time. Then I found out how many people we actually knew in the Roussillon, because every few days I was greeted by someone I knew. A friend or a musician, a father of a kid in our son's class, a fan of John's who lived in our village, a woman that Julie had met when she had gone out to do tango dancing one night during her stay with us... The world was smaller than it seemed and the network around John was tighter than I think he'd ever thought. John had never felt very much at home in the Roussillon, but in this period, it turned out many people were on his side.

John had a roommate and he talked with him and his wife Marie-Claude about music. He asked her to sing French folk songs and one of those songs he liked particularly. "It's a nice melody, can you sing that again?"

Marie-Claude had been talking to John when he was still in a coma, saying hello, goodbye. She was nice but also a bit talkative. And John loved silence....

One day we were talking with just the two of us, when John said:

"I think I did something wrong: I told Marie-Claude to shut up..."

"Oops! What happened?"

"... then they were silent, mumbling."

"Did you say you were sorry?"

"Yes. And I said that when all this is over, we should go out for dinner together."

"Yes, that's a good idea!"

"They were saying oh no, it was too expensive and stuff."

"We'll figure it all out, by then."

I was amazed to hear John say he'd apologized. He never used to say sorry for outbursts like that. It felt as if he was saying one big sorry for all the times when he'd been too rough on people. A week after that, he couldn't talk any more. But the sorry had been said.

From lying in bed, unable to move for so long, John had developed a back sore and he may already have had the beginnings of a bone infection. He must have been in great pain. He often wanted to stand up to take the pressure off but due to the stroke, he wasn't allowed to. In hindsight I understand he lost his temper... and he found it back.

In all this, John didn't forget about playing music. One day we were talking about the drummer Don Moye, who had called to ask how he was doing and who sent him well-wishes. Don was now living in Marseille, three hours away.

John: "Wasn't I supposed to have a concert with him soon?"
Me: "Yes, that would be in three weeks from now. We cancelled it."
"Oh... why?"
"We were thinking you weren't well enough for it yet..."
John, sad and disappointed: "Oh... but I can play softly..."

At the cremation ceremony, Don Moye played congas for John.

Many musicians played at a memorial ceremony in Copenhagen, Denmark.

Friends in our village of Claira gave a new street his name: Rue John Tchicai.

The next summer Julie came down from Denmark. We rented a motorboat and sailed up the Mediterranean. There we dispersed John's ashes into the blue water.

Whale respiration

In the spring of '95, on a nice day in California, we took a trip to the coast. People said it was a good time for whale watching, and this year the whales were meandering from their regular route. They were closer to the coast than usual.

We drove to San Francisco and down southwards. In the late afternoon, we checked into a hotel in Daly City, and went towards the ocean for a stroll.

Daly City had a pier that ran into the sea for about 200 metres. It was beginning to get dark when we were out on the pier, together with other people. People said the whales were very close to the shore and it was true, because sometimes we heard sounds and saw big, dark shapes come up from out of the water, visible for just a second and then they disappeared.

We stood there and watched. All of a sudden, a whale came up just in front of us. It was breathing out. That sounded like a horse's neighing, only much stronger. The whale was enormous, it was the size of a school bus and its movement was amazing. In just a few seconds it came up from out of the water, we saw an eye, we heard its breath, and then it went down again. It felt like a moment of close contact with eternity. We didn't see the whale again. The next morning we came back with our photo camera in hand, but of course there was no whale to be seen.

At the end of his life, John was in the intensive care unit of a hospital. He was connected to many machines, and a respiratory aid machine was one of them. There was no hope that he would recover and we asked the doctors to help him transit to the hereafter. Palliative care was given. One of the crucial questions was, what would happen after the disconnection from the breathing machine? Would his body succumb immediately or could John still breathe by himself?

I was holding my breath while the doctor turned off the machine and removed the tube from John's nose…, and then I heard the whale come back. Very slowly, John took a very deep in-breath, and after a pause, he gave a very long out-breath. The doctor and I were relieved.

As John continued his long and deep breathing, I was thinking he must be happy to be freed from the machine and able to breathe on his own. He had spent many years of his life doing breathing exercises through yoga. Breath was very important to him. I had often witnessed him practising, but this breathing was the longest, the quietest and the most peaceful I'd ever heard. It was still strong. Listening to it calmed me down. I began to feel my tiredness and rested my head on his right hand. "Hands that can uproot a tree", journalist David Rubian of the San Francisco Chronicle *had written once. John's hand was big and warm, and it made me feel safe just like it had done so many times before.*

John's last teaching session, at a masterclass for
psychologists at the CETT in Vejle. Denmark, November
2011

Appendix 1: Advice to improvisers

John's philosophy behind the process of learning improvisation was specific, and his teaching method was very precise and concrete. He described it in his book "Advice to improvisers", published in Denmark in 1987 by Edition Wilhelm Hansen. The book is still available in print. It contains composition charts, musical exercices and Advice.

The following is an illustration of the Advice-section of the book.

John distinguished four basic steps you should take for learning how to improvise:

1. **Listen** - ear training, imitate what you hear.
2. **Create** - form your own phrase/motif/ostinato
3. **Improvise** - make variations on existing elements
4. **Play together** with other people - communicate

He explained these steps as follows:

1. **Listening skills** *"are essential in order to learn to coordinate the ear with the action of the instrument, and to learn to execute on the instrument what is being played to you or what you hear in your inner ear. Developing this ability is necessary for a creative improviser and it applies to people in the jazz field and for classically trained musicians it is an absolute must."*

2. With a trained and awakened inner ear, students can begin to **create** and compose their own phrases. During workshops John used to give exercices with ostinato motifs:

"One at the time, the students play or sing a phrase that they can repeat exactly. Three, six, nine or more times.

Each phrase can be repeated by the group as a whole or by smaller groups within the group. The main point is that they are created on the spot, either from inner inspiration or by inspiration coming from listening to the other groups."

3. After having created one thing, the next step is to make variations on it, to play it again but differently, and to do so on the spot. Then it becomes **improvisation.**

"Such an ostinato phrase can be the point of departure for another form of improvisation. This form is based on the germs of the chosen phrase, and it is up to the creativity and sense of structure of the student which direction the improvisation will take. "

If the ostinato (or other starting element) has a clear tonal center, it can lead to improvisation in a certain key and perhaps one can create chords to it. If the ostinato is very rhythmic, it can lead to a more rhythmical improvisation by playing with that rhythm, creating counter rhythms to it, etc... Possibilities are endless.

John explains the basic variation technique he used for composition:
"Let's say we have created this line:

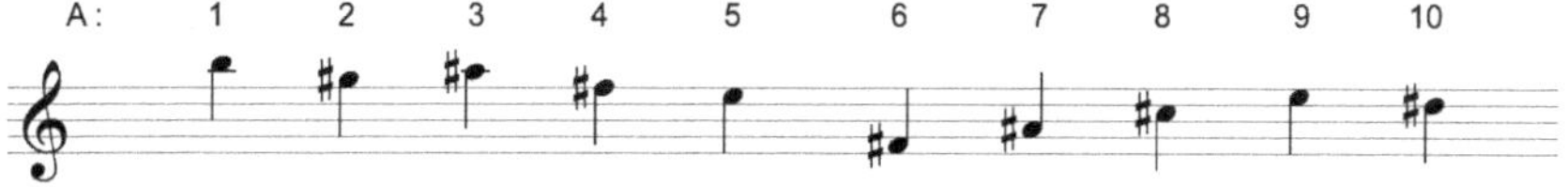

This line contains the germ cells for the further development of the composition, and by changing the notes around, it is possible to make many different variations on this basic material. We can give numbers to each note on line A.

Then by giving new numbers to the notes on line B, we get the first variation of the original row of notes:

The new variation will look like this:

It is possible to do the same thing using each interval as a unit:

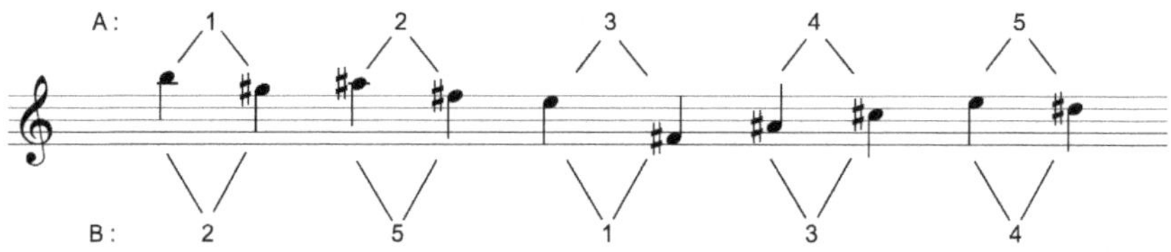

And *by transposing the lines, or some of them, one gets again new possibilities.*

If the musician understands this principle and is able to work with this very useful tool in his improvisations, it is indeed to his advantage.
The rhythmical aspect and the arrangement of the sounds in time are not dealt with in this example."

© Edition Wilhelm Hansen, Copenhagen.
All Rights Reserved. International Copyright Secured.
Used with kind permission of Hal Leonard Europe Limited.

4. **Playing together** with others.

A musician can play on his own, but of course playing together with other people offers more diverse sound possibilites. In his book John gives advice on how to make playing together with other musicians a pleasant experience, both musically and socially. His focus here is on playing free improvisation, but some of it also counts for playing music together in general.

- He recommends to not start playing all at once, but one person at a time. This person determines the mood of the piece through his choice of tones and the way of playing them. Each person that joins, plays in response or in accompaniment to what the first person is playing.
- Unexperienced players should try to make the improvisation simple, meaning not too many different notes and not too sophisticated rhythms. *It's better to play many short improvisations with a variety in structure and a variety in tasks and roles rather than to play long improvisations.*
- *Test yourself in hearing two things at once, hearing your own playing while at the same time being aware of what your colleague in the group is playing. He might be trying to get in touch with you by playing certain signals which you possibly don't hear, either because you play too loud and your sensitivity is deafened, or simply you have not trained your mind in polyrhythmic/melodic activity. It is important to be modest and not too egoistic when you play music together with others. In free improvisation the player should keep lots of space open where he doesn't play but just listens to the others.*
- *Modesty is also important concerning the soloist's role. Don't always take the role of a virtuosic soloist, letting the other players serve as accompaniment partners for you. Instead, you should also take the role of the accompanist, being modest enough to accept this role which is of no less importance.*
  Strangely enough, it is by playing accompaniment that you learn much about how to develop a solo. It is in this function that you can test your ability of rhythmic drive, precision, intensity, and tempo steadiness. The steady tempo concerns all improvisers, but when you play accompaniment and something is wrong with the tempo and it is not under control, if it slows down or becomes faster and the

accompanists are not able to secure steadiness of tempo in a certain piece, it will be a disaster for the group and the music.

© Edition Wilhelm Hansen, Copenhagen.
All Rights Reserved. International Copyright Secured.
Used with kind permission of Hal Leonard Europe Limited.

Impression of a John Tchicai workshop; cartoon by a French participant. Denmark 1985

Appendix 2: Some examples of John's more experimental performances

<u>New York Museum of Modern Art, July 1965:</u>
John Tchicai paints his face for a performance by the New York Art Quartet

<u>Copenhagen, 1968:</u>
Cadentia Nova Danica performs free jazz for young people at dance venues

<u>Rungsted, 1975:</u>
School concert with John's students playing music while birds, in cages, are singing on stage

<u>"Frobenius Stomp" on *Live in Athens*, 1980:</u>
During a solo concert, John performs with the audience. He begins with question and answer in improvised singing and clapping, then John starts improvising on saxophone to the audience's clapping and singing. After five minutes of changes in tone color and dynamics, it ends with a long applause and laughter. John says "OK, the singing lesson is over!" and continues with a song on the saxophone

<u>Copenhagen, early '80s:</u>
Concert with three players in front of a screen and John sitting behind it. Musicians play on cues given by John pulling strings attached to their arms

<u>Huset, Copenhagen, '80s:</u>
Five players behind a curtain throw fishes over the curtain into the
room, then they come on stage making dance movements and playing
their instruments

<u>Davis, California 1992:</u>
Participatory slideshow for audience and musicians
The audience, divided in two groups and watching slides with images or text, recite the text and are silent during images, accompanied
by a group of musicians who improvise freely on the audience's
sounds. Slideshow created by John Tchicai

Appendix 3: Making a setlist

When John was deciding the order of the compositions to be played at a concert, he tried to have a smooth flow between the pieces and was always very concerned with the transitions between them. He had a method to go about it.

He spread out all the charts in front of him on the floor. For pieces he played by heart and for free improvisations, he took a blank sheet of paper with just the title written on it. Then he chose one piece to start with and played the beginning of it. If it felt good he kept that as the opening piece. Then he played the ending of the piece and listened to the silence after it. Based on how that sounded, he chose a piece to follow that silence. Then he played the ending of the first piece followed by the beginning of this next one and listened whether it made for a good transition in rhythm, mood or tonality. If it worked, he took its sheet of paper and put it after the first piece. But sometimes it didn't work as a second piece, and then he repeated the process with another composition.

It could take a while until the set list was ready, but this procedure offered a bit of a guarantee that the music would flow naturally and organically during the concert. This way he composed the whole set as a big collage.

Appendix 4: Music chart examples

All compositions ©John Tchicai/KODA

The task at hand

m + w John Tchicai

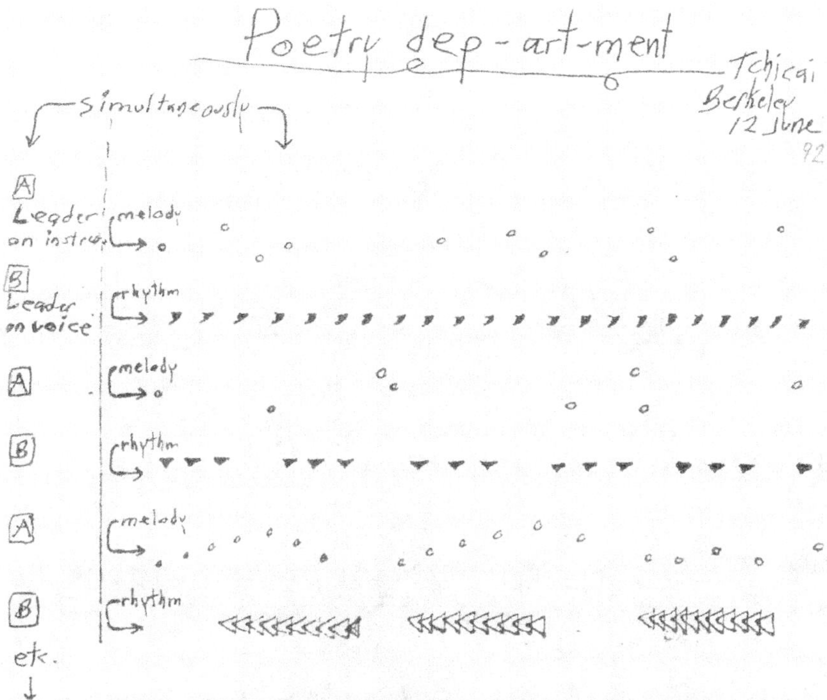

Explanation: When leader plays instrumentally, group plays short tones with long spaces in between, try to anticipate and play some of the same tones in the same moment as other players would do them. In B: When leader sings, do repetitive rhythms, on one tone only.

Eb Alto

That one for whom?

Approximate transcription of the first part of John Tchicai's solo alto saxophone playing in the same-titled composition on LP "Live in Athens", 1980

transcribed by Margriet Naber

Bb Tenor

Love is touching

*Transcription of John Tchicai's solo tenor saxophone playing
in introduction of this piece
as recorded on the CD "Love is Touching"*

transcribed by Margriet Naber

Tempo ad lib

All-embracing space

w John Tchicai / m J.Tchicai & M.Naber '96

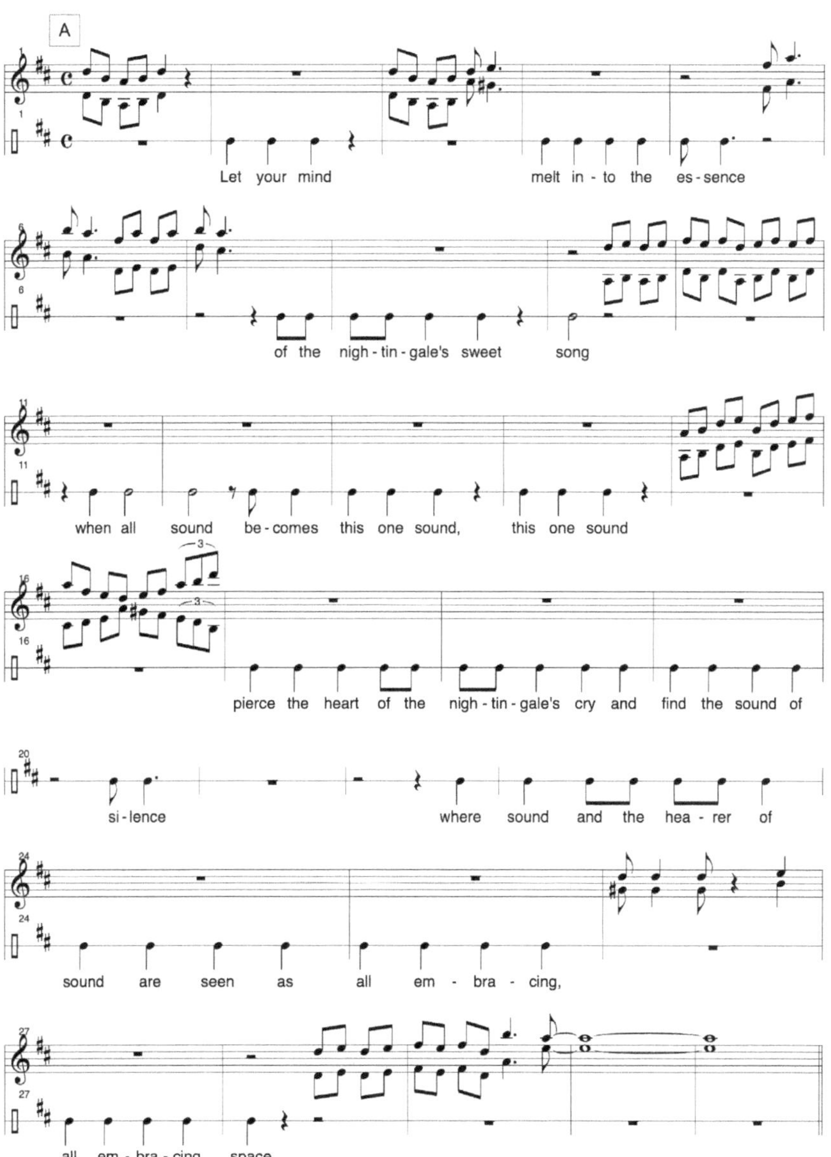

Appendix 5: Discography

Detailed Listing of Issues (year of recording listed in parenthesis). Compiled by Erik Raben.

- *Jazz Jamboree 1962, vol. 4*, Jørgen Leth Quintet (1962) - Muza(P) 0397
- *Rufus*, John Tchicai, Archie Shepp, J.C.Moses, Don Moore (1963) - Fontana(Eu) 681.014ZL
- *Consequences*, New York Contemporary Five (1963) - Fontana(Eu) 681.013ZL
- *Jazz In Denmark*, (var. artists) (1963) - Marshmallow(J) MMEX-DVD101(DVD)
- *Live At Jazzhus Montmartre, Vol.1*, New York Contemporary Five (1963) - Sonet(D) SLP36, identical to Archie Shepp In Europe *New York Contemporary Five, vol. 1* - Delmark DL409 and Storyville's *Archie Shepp + the New York Contemporary Five,* 21.016
- *Live At Jazzhus Montmartre, Vol.2*, New York Contemporary Five (1963) - Sonet(D) SLP51, identical to Archie Shepp In Europe *New York Contemporary Five, vol. 2* (1963) - Delmark DL412 (possibly unissued) and Storyville's *Archie Shepp with the New York Contemporary Five* STCD 8209/101.8385.
- *Bill Dixon Septet/Archie Shepp And The New York Contemporary Five,* (1964) - Savoy MG12184
- *New York Eye And Ear Control* (1964) - ESP 1016
- *Four For Trane*, Archie Shepp (1964) - Impulse A(S)71
- *Call It Art*, New York Art Quartet – (1964/65) Triple Point TPR 16(5xLP)

- *New York Art Quartet,* New York Art Quartet (1964) - ESP 1004,1004-2 (CD)
- *Communication,* Jazz Composers' Orchestra (1964) - Fontana(Eu) 681.011ZL
- *Ascension,* John Coltrane(1965) - Impulse A(S) 95/543.413-2 (CD)
- *Mohawk,* New York Art Quartet (1965) - Fontana(Eu) 681.009ZL
- *Old Stuff,* New York Art Quartet (1965) - Cuneiform RUNE300 (CD)
- *Roswell Rudd,* New York Art Quartet (1965) - America(F) 30AM6114
- *August 1966 Jazzhus Montmartre,* Cadentia Nova Danica (1967) - Storyville(D) 101.8441 (CD)
- *Instant Composers Pool,* Han Bennink–Misha Mengelberg–John Tchicai (1968) - ICP (Du) 002
- *Instant Composers Pool* (var. artists) (1968-77) - ICP(Du) 1275 (52xCD + 2xDVD)
- *John Tchicai & Cadentia Nova Danica* (1968) - Polydor(Eu) 583.770
- *Unfinished Music #2 –Life With The Lions,* John Lennon & Yoko Ono (1969) - Zapple(E)01 Rykodisc RCD10412 (CD)
- *M144,* Burnin Red Ivanhoe (1969) Sonet(D) - SLPS1512/13, SLP1618(2xLP)
- *Afrodisiaca,* John Tchicai & Cadentia Nova Danica (1969) - MPS(G) 15249
- *Fragments,* Han Bennink–Misha Mengelberg–J. Tchicai–Derek Bailey (1970) - ICP (Du)005
- *ICP Double,* Willem Breuker: (1970)ICP(Du)008
- *Music For His Films (1967-1978),* Johan van der Keuken - Willem Breuker - BV Haast(Du)015, CD9709/9710 (2xCD)
- *Wiebelfetzer Live* (1971) - Bazillus(Sw) ZILL111/112(2xLP)

- *Monster Sticksland Meeting Two,* George Gruntz (1974) - MPS(G)15427 John Tchicai Quartet (1974) Emanem(E) 3317 (unissued)
- *Live At Willisau Jazz Festival,* John Tchicai–Irène Schweizer Group (1975) - Willisau Live(Sw)WIL1, Atavistic Unheard Music Ser.UMS/ALP210(CD)
- *God In Africa,* John Tchicai And The Festival Band (1976) - Hookfarm (D) HCDS76-8 (2xCD)
- *John Tchicai Solo Plus Albert Mangelsdorf* (1977) - FMP(G) SAJ12
- *Darktown Highlights,* John Tchicai & Strange Brothers (1977) - Storyville(D) SLP1015
- *Darktown Highlights/Put Up The Fight,* John Tchicai (1977/ 1987) - Storyville(D) 103.8431 (2xCD)
- *Real Tchicai,* John Tchicai (1977) - SteepleChase(D) SCCD31075(CD)
- *I.C.P. Tentet in Berlin* (1977) - FMP(G)SAJ23
- *Workshop Freie Musik – For Example,* (var. artists)(1977) FMP(G)R1-3(3xLP)
- *The Kabul And Teheran Tapes,* Hartmut Geerken –John Tchicai (1977) - Qbico(I) QBICO87 (2xLP)
- *Tetterettet,* I.C.P. Tentet (1977) - ICP(Du) 020
- *John Tchicai & Strange Brothers* (1977) - FMP(G) SAJ15
- *Duets,* John Tchicai –André Goudbeek (1977) - SVM(B)2
- *Witchdoctor's Son,* Johnny Dyani (1978) - SteepleChase(D) SCS1098/SCCD31098 (CD)
- *Who's Who,* The Berlin JazzWorkshop Orchestra (1978) - FMP(G) SAJ24
- *Barefoot,* John Tchicai –André Goudbeek (1977) - Marge(F)07
- *Darn It!* Paul Haines (1979/1990) - American Clavé AMCL1014/1018 (2xCD)
- *Ballad Round The Left Corner,* Pierre Dørge Quartet (1979) - SteepleChase(D) SCCD31132 (CD)

- *Musical Monsters,* Cherry –Tchicai –Schweizer –Francioli –Favre (1980) - Intakt(Sw) CD269 (CD)
- *Continent,* John Tchicai –Hartmut Geerken (1980) - Praxis(Gr) CM102
- *Live In Athens,* John Tchicai (1980) - Praxis(Gr) CM101
- *Den yderste ø,* Yggdrasil –Digte af William Heinesen (1981) Tutl(Faroese) HJF12/HJF12(CD)
- *Yes Please,* Chris McGregor's Brotherhood of Breath (1981) - In and Out(F) IAO100
- *Ball At Louisiana,* John Tchicai –Pierre Dørge (1981) - SteepleChase(D) SCCD31174 (CD)
- *Pierre Dørge & New Jungle Orchestra* (1982) - SteepleChase(D) SCCD31162 (CD)
- *Ravnating,* Yggdrasil (1982) - Tutl(Faroese) HJF13/HJF13 (CD)
- *Askur,* Yggdrasil (1982-2003) - Tutl(Faroese) HJF133 (2xCD)
- *Binder Quintet Featuring John Tchicai* (1982) - Krém(Hu) SLPX17759
- *Spiritual Jazz –Vol. 3* European (var. artists) (1982) Jazzman(E) JMANLP050/JMANCD050 (CD)
- *Merlin Vibrations* Hot Channels –John Tchicai Orchestra (1983) Plainisphare(Sw) PL1267-10
- *Heygar og Dreygar,* Yggdrasil (1983) Tutl(Faroese) HJF15
- *The Four Towers & Heygar og Dreygar* Yggdrasil (1983,1985) Tutl(Faroese) HJF15/19 (CD)
- *Timo's Message,* John Tchicai Group (1984) - Black Saint(I) 120094-1/120094-2 (CD)
- *Brikama,* Pierre Dørge & New Jungle Orchestra (1984) - SteepleChase(D) SCCD31188 (CD)
- *Concerto Grotto,* Kristian Blak (1984) - Tutl(Faroese) HJF18
- *Winged Serpent (Sliding Quadrants),* Cecil Taylor (1984) - Soul Note(I) SN1089 BXS1007 (5xCD)

- *The African Tapes, vol. 1 & 2*, Moye-Tchicai-Geerken (1985) - Praxis(Gr)CM114/5Golden Years(E) GY9/10 (2xCD)
- *Cassava Balls*, Moye-Tchicai-Geerken (1985) - Praxis(Gr) CM111/Golden Years(E) GY4 (CD)
- *De fire tårne*, Yggdrasil (1985) - Tutl(Faroese) HJF19
- *Angolian Cry*, Johnny Dyani (1985) - SteepleChase(D) SCS1209/SCCD31209 (CD)
- *Even The Moon Is Dancing*, Pierre Dørge & New Jungle Orchestra (1985) - SteepleChase(D) SCS1208/SCCD31208 (CD)
- *Live At Bim And More*, De Zes Winden/The Six Winds (1986) - BVHaast(Du) 064
- *Johnny Lives*, Pierre Dørge & New Jungle Orchestra (1987) - SteepleChase(D) SCCD31228(CD)
- *Soaked Sorrows*, Brus Trio With John Tchicai (1987) - Dragon(Sd) DRLP16
- *Put Up The Fight*, John Tchicai Group (1987) - Storyville(D) SLP4141
- *The Giancarlo Nicolai Trio And John Tchicai*, (1987) - Leo(E) CDLR164(CD)
- *Letter to South Africa*, Curtis Clark (1987) - Nimbus NS501(CD)
- *Tchicai / Clinch*, (1988) - Olufsen(D) DOC5071
- *Always Born*, Charles Gayle Quartet feat. John Tchicai (1988) - Silkheart(Sd) SHCD115(CD)
- *Brøytingar*, Yggdrasil (1988) - Tutl(Faroese) HJF21(CD)
- *Elephants Can Dance*, De Zes Winden/The Six Winds (1988) - Sackville(Ca) 3041
- *Different Places, Different Bananas*, Pierre Dørge & New Jungle Orchestra (1988) - Olufsen(D) DOCD5079 (CD)
- *Peer Gynt*, Pierre Dørge & New Jungle Orchestra (1989) Olufsen(D) DOC5094/DOCD5207 (CD)
- *Man Met Muts*, De Zes Winden/The Six Winds (1989) - BVHaast(Du) CD9004 (CD)

- *Live In Chicago,* Pierre Dørge & New Jungle Orchestra (1990) - Olufsen(D) DOCD5122(CD)
- *Anybody Home?,* John Tchicai (1990/2000) - Tutl(Faroese) HJF76(CD)
- *Satisfaction,* John Tchicai –Vitold Rek (1991) Enja(G) 7033-2(CD) Art Of The Duo, vol. 1 (var. artists) (1991) Enja(G) 8008-2(CD)
- *2 x 2,* John Tchicai –Vitold Rek –Karl Berger (1991/92) - Taso (G) TCM505(CD)
- *Anger Dance,* De Zes Winden (1991/92) - BVHaast (Du) CD9305(CD)
- *Grandpa's Spells,* John Tchicai Quartet feat. Misha Mengelberg (1992) - Storyville(D) STCD4182(CD)
- *Aouda,* Peter Danstrup (1992) - Olufsen(D) DOCD5189(CD)
- *Wavelength Infinity: A Sun Ra Tribute* (var. artists) (1994) - Rastascan BRD018 (2xCD).
- *Love Is Touching,* John Tchicai And The Archetypes (1994) B&W BW055(CD)
- *Music With No Name, Volume One* (var. artists) (1994) - B&W BW080 (CD)
- *Ancient Civilizations,* Francisco Mondragon Rio (1994) - Pulque PULCD6(CD)
- *Ulterior Motif,* Mat Marucci: (1995) Jazz Inspiration 9320(CD)
- *John Ehlis Ensemble,* John Ehlis Ensemble (1995) - Sivac 1001(CD)
- *Ok Nok ... Kongo + Three Jokers Plays Thomas Agergaard & John Tchicai* (1996) - Storyville(D) STCD4220(CD)
- *Adapt ....or Die!* Rent Romus' Lords Of Outland –John Tchicai (1996/97) - Jazzheads JH9503(CD)
- *Manestraal,* De Zes Winden (1997) BVHaast (Du) CD9706(CD)
- Vision Volume One: Vision Festival 1997" Compiled (var. artists) - Aum Fidelity AUM007/8(2xCD)

- *Love Notes From The Madhouse,* John Tchicai–Yusef Komunyakaa (1997) - 8thHarmonic Breakdown 8THHB80001(CD)
- *"Giraf,* Pierre Dørge & New Jungle Orchestra (1998) - Dacapo(D) DCCD9440 (CD)
- *Dansk musik i 1000 år–Jazz* (var. artists) (1998/99) - Dacapo(D) 8.224196(CD)
- *Life Overflowing,* John Tchicai –Charlie Kohlhase (1998) - Nada Music 001(CD)
- *Moonstone Journey,* Ok Nok ... Kongo (1998/99) - Dacapo(D) DCCD9444(CD)
- *35th Reunion,* New York Art Quartet (1999) - DIW(J) DIW936(CD)
- *San Carlos,* John Ehlis (1999) - Sivac 1002(CD)
- *Infinitesimal Flash,* John Tchicai (1999) - Buzz ZZ76010(CD)
- *Ups & Downs,* Matchbrothers feat. John Tchicai & Pierre Dørge (1999) - Cope(D) COPECD101(CD)
- *Yo Miles!: Sky Garden,* Henry Kaiser (2000) - Cuneiform Rune 191/192(2xCD)
- *Yo Miles Project: Upriver,* Henry Kaiser (2000) - Cuneiform Rune 201/202(2xCD)
- *On Top Of Your Head* John Tchicai (2001) - Ninth World Music(D) NWM025(CD)
- *Hymne Til Sofia,* J.Tchicai –Kr.Høeg –Ib Bindel & Musica Sacra Nova (2001) - Calibrated(D) CALI012CD)
- *The Polish Folk Explosion,* Vitold Rek–Kapela Resovian (2001) Taso (G) TMP507(CD)
- *The 25th Ninth World Music Release,* (var. artists)(2001) Ninth World Music(D) NWM025(CD)
- *ComPOsed,* Lou Grassi's Po Band and John Tchicai (2002) - CIMP262(CD)
- *Fo(u)r Beings,* Adam Lane (2002) - CIMP263(CD)
- *Sudden Happiness,* Triot –John Tchicai (2002) - TUM(Fi) CD008(CD)

- *Dos,* Adam Lane –John Tchicai (2002) - CIMP278(CD)
- *Hope is Bright Green Up North,* J.Tchicai –Pierre Dørge –Lou Grassi (2002) - CIMP281 (CD)
- *Oliver Lake –John Tchicai –Jonas Westergaard –Kresten Osgood* (2003) - Passin' Thru 41224(CD)
- *Big Chief Dreaming,* J.Tchicai –Garrison Fewell –Tino Tracanna 5tet (2003) - Soul Note(I) 121.385-2(CD)
- *Set lyd: J. Tchicai –Musik/ Arne Ærtebjerg –Digte,* Oda Knudsen (2003) - Clausens Kunsthandel(D) unnumbered (CD)
- *Good Night Songs,* John Tchicai –Charlie Kohlhase –Garrison Fewell (2003) - Boxholder 050/051 (2xCD)
- *Witch's Scream,* John Tchicai –Andrew Cyrille –Reggie Workman (2004) - TUM CD014 (CD)
- *John Tchicai With Strings,* John Tchicai –Spring Heel Jack (2005) - Treader(E) TRD005 (CD)
- *Clapham Duos,* John Tchicai –Evan Parker (2005) - Treader(E) TRD022 (CD)
- Consul Pepsi & The Sweet Thunder Poetry Parade (2006) - Buchanan(D) BR003 (CD)
- *Boiler,* The All Ear Trio (2006) - Ninth World Music(D) NWM038 (CD)
- *Triplepoint,* Stefan Pasborg (2006) - Ilk Music(D) ILK130 (3xCD)
- *Tribal Ghost,* John Tchicai –Kohlhase –Fewell –McBee –Hart (2007)- NoBusiness NBLP65
- *Letter From America,* Paul Hemmings Trio with John Tchicai (2007) - Leading Tone LTR07.003 (CD)
- *Songs & Themes,* Spring Heel Jack (Ashley Wales –John Coxon) (2007) - Thirsty Ear(E)57183 (CD)
- *ELEKTRO featuring John Tchicai,* ELEKTRO (2007/2010) - Blackout Music(D) 032 (CD)
- *Coltrane In Spring,* Tchicai/Müller/Munch-Hansen/Osgood (2007) - ILK(D)141 (CD)

- *No Trespassing,* John Tchicai + Ice9 (2007) - Azzurra(I) TBP11472 (CD)
- *One Long Minute,* John Tchicai's Five Points (2008) - Nu Bop NB007 (CD)
- *Treader Duos,* Butcher & Sanders / Ward & Turner / Tchicai & Marsh (2008) - Treader(E) TRD013 (CD)
- *The Truth Lies In-Between,* John Tchicai (2008) - Hôte Marge(F) 01 (CD)
- *Spiritual Man –Live at Ceglie Jazz Open Fest.* Open Orch.–J.Tchicai (2008) - Terre Sommerse(I) TS-JEI008 (CD)
- *Look to the Neutrino,* John Tchicai Lunar Quartet (2008) - Music Center(I) BA243 (CD)
- *In Monk's Mood,* John Tchicai (2008) - SteepleChase(D) SCCD31675 (CD)
- *Blues In Green, Yellow, Red,* Bjørn Bech-John Tchicai (2009) - Ninth World Music(D) NWM04 (CD)
- *Live at the Moro Jazz Festival,* Franco Ferguson –John Tchicai (2009) - Franco Ferguson(I) 2011 (CD)
- *Reptiles In The Sky,* Peter Danstrup (2009 - Gateway DAN-PETCD01 (CD)
- *Dell –Westergaard–Lillinger Feat. John Tchicai* (2010) - Jazzwerkstatt(G) JW128 (CD)
- *Along The Way,* John Ehlis (2010) - Sivac 1003 (CD)
- *Men From Windy Land,* Stefano Maltese –John Tchicai (2010) - Labirinti Sonori(I) LS014(CD)
- *Dødens Garderobe feat. John Tchicai,* Dødens Garderobe (2011) - Barefoot(D) BFREC020 (CD)
- *Other Violets,* The Engines w/John Tchicai (2011) - Not Two MW 895-2 (CD)
- *Beautiful Untrue Things,* Peter Danstrup –Reptiles (2011) - Gateway DANPETCD02 (CD)
- *Long Story Short,* Peter Brötzmann (2011) - Trost Records(A) TR112 (5xCD)

- *Message Of Love,* Katrine Suwalski Another World (2011) - Gateway(D) KATSUW005 (CD)

MARGRIET NABER

Acknowledgements

"Of course, write that book about John! He was one of the important figures on the Danish jazz scene. There have been books written about less important personalities in Danish music, so, of course you should do that. Do that!" Saxophonist Karsten Vogel said this to me during our interview a few years ago, and finally I can say: Karsten, I did it!

The interviews with him and with all other musicians and friends and students of John's were very inspiring. Talking with them was fun and, their contributions helped form this book. Thanks to you all.

Many thanks to my 'predecessors': to the women who were married to John before I was, first of all Kirsten Iversen, dear friend-sister-co-mother of John's children. Marianne Lassen, the artist, and Annette Sidenius, the resolute woman, have unfortunately passed away in the years I spent working on this book, but eternal thanks go to you. You helped me understand John better and you were a support in difficult times.

Thanks to Karen Hill Anton who helped make a connection to Annette and encouraged me to write and self-publish my story.

Enormous thanks to Richard Williams who read, edited and fact-checked the text and improved the book's structure. His support, expertise and knowledge were invaluable.

Many thanks to the photographers who kindly let me use their expressive photos in this book. Photos not credited in by-lines are part of the family archive, or its photographer could not be traced: if anyone feels miscredited, please contact me.

Great thanks to Erik Raben who meticulously gathered data to compile the discography of all of John's recordings.

Many thanks to my dear 'panel members' Alan Roth, Russ Tucker, Charlie Kohlhase, and John Coxon, who were always willing to answer questions.

Thanks to Joep Schillings, who congratulated me every time I finished writing a new part. I promised I would thank you in the book, well: here you go!

Thanks to my brother-in-law Joe Hoey, for his patient tech help and assistance.

Thanks to Georgia Vasilaras whose critical ear, talent with words and loving help I can count on in many aspects of life.

Many thanks to my dear sister Jonneke, who encouraged me to keep writing after she first read about "the sound field coming to a rest with a fade-out" in the introduction. Now, she tells me in Dutch to "put a dot behind it", which means it's time to finish writing and present John Tchicai's biography to the world.

Thanks, John. Thanks very much.

Margriet Naber
April 2021

Sources

Barnett, Anthony. *"UnNatural Music: John Lennon & Yoko Ono in Cambridge 1969: Account of the Circumstances Surrounding Their Appearance at the Natural Music Concert"*. Lewes, East Sussex: Allardyce Book ABP, 2016

Braad Thomsen, Christian. *"Blues for Montmartre"*. Copenhagen: Kollektiv Film, 2011

Fewell, Garrison . *"Outside Music, Inside Voices - dialogues on improvisation and the spirit of creative music"*. Somerville, MA: Saturn University Press 2014

Hamilton, Andy. *"Lee Konitz, conversations on the Improviser's Art"*. Ann Arbor, MI: The University of Michigan Press, 2007

Høeg, TS. "Virkeligheden blænder, hvis man ser den, som den er". *Jazzspecial* #130, dec 2012/jan 2013

"In Memoriam: John Tchicai 1936-2012". New York: *The New York City Jazz Record*, December 2012 - No. 128

"Kaj Timmermann Biografi". Danskefilm.dk. 05 April 2021 <https://danskefilm.dk/skuespiller.php?id=8689>

McEachrane, Michael. "The Midnight Sun Never Sets: An Email Conversation About Jazz, Race and National Identity in Denmark, Norway and Sweden" edited by Michael McEachrane. *"Afro-Nordic Landscapes - Equality and Race in Northern Europe"*, New York/London. Routledge, Taylor & Francis Group, 2014

Meyer, Cim. "Den gådefulde Tchicai", an interview with Pierre Dørge. *Jazzspecial* #130, dec 2012/jan 2013

Morgenstern, Dan. "John Tchicai: a calm member of the avantgarde". *Downbeat,* February 10, 1966.

Naber, Margriet. Interviews with Anthony Barnett (2020), Irene Becker (2015), Han Bennink (2017), Peter Bennink (2017), Preben Brandsborg (2018), Bent Clausen (2015), John Coxon (2019), Peter Danstrup (2015), Pierre Dørge (2015), Thorsten Høeg (2015), Niels Holt (2018), Bodil Høyer (2017), Kirsten Iversen (2019), François Jeanneau (2018), Anders Kirkegaard (2015), Charlie Kohlhase (2018), Marianne Lassen (2015), Anders Lassen (2015), Stine Lassen (2015), Don Moyé (2019), Makaya Ntshoko (2012), Kresten Osgood (2015), Ole Rømer (2015), Irene Schweizer (2012), Archie Shepp (2018), Annette Sidenius (2012), Diane Sosnoski (2020), Simon Spang-Hanssen (2015), Katrine Suwalski (2015), Mauritz Tchikai (2015), Michel Tignères (2019), Karsten Vogel (2018).

Naber, Margriet. E-mail exchanges with Oliver Lake (2018) and Marte Röling (2019)

Rasmussen, Lars. *"Mbizo - A book about Johnny Dyani"*. Copenhagen: The Booktrader, 2003

Rømer, Ole. "Nærværet var et kendetegn" *Jazzspecial* #130, dec 2012/jan 2013

Roth, Alan. *"The breath courses through us"*. New York: Asymmetric Pictures, 2013

Skovgaard, Ib. "John Tchicai - playing the alto like a metal poem". *Jazzspecial* #130, dec 2012/jan 2013

Steinmetz, Hugh. "Free Jazz i 1960erne". *Jazzspecial* #130, dec 2012/jan 2013

Tchicai, John. "132 Observational Measurements" (recorded for NDR in Eldenaer Jazz Evenings, Greifswald, Germany, 1995 - not published on record yet).

Tchicai, John. "A chaos with some kind of order". *Moonstone Journey*, Ok Nok ... Kongo (1998/99) - Dacapo DCCD9444

Tchicai, John. "All-embracing space". Not published on record yet. © John Tchicai, KODA-Denmark

Tchicai, John. Liner notes, *Love is Touching*, John Tchicai and the Archetypes (1994) B&W BW055

Tchicai, John. "Love is Touching", transcription by Margriet Naber. *Love is Touching,* John Tchicai and the Archetypes (1994) B&W BW055

Tchicai, John. Liner notes. *Mohawk,* New York Art Quartet (1965) - Fontana(Eu) 681.009ZL

Tchicai, John. "Monk's Dream" *Witch's Scream,* John Tchicai - Andrew Cyrille - Reggie Workman (2004) - TUM CD014 (CD)

Tchicai, John. "Poetry Dep-Art-Ment" *Love is Touching,* John Tchicai and the Archetypes (1994) B&W BW055

Tchicai, John. "Satisfaction". *Satisfaction,* John Tchicai - Vitold Rek (1991) Enja 7033-2

Tchicai, John. "The bass is the base". *Satisfaction,* John Tchicai - Vitold Rek (1991) Enja 7033-2

Tchicai, John. "That one for whom?" transcription by Margriet Naber. *Live In Athens,* John Tchicai (1980) - Praxis CM101

Tchicai, John *"The task at hand".* Not published on record yet. © John Tchicai, KODA-Denmark

Ulrich, Torben. *"Jazz, bold & buddhisme".* Edited by Lars Movin. Copenhagen: Informations Forlag, 2003

Wiedemann, Erik. *Live At Jazzhus Montmartre, Vol. 1 New York Contemporary Five,* liner notes, New York Contemporary Five (1963) - Sonet(D) SLP36

Young, Ben & Lizzi, Joe. *"Call it Art".* New York: Triple Point, 2013

Other resources for John Tchicai's music

A lot of info can be found on www.johntchicai.com.

The manuscripts of John Tchicai's compositions and his reel-to-reel tapes can be consulted at the Royal Danish Library, Søren Kierkegaards Plads 1, 1221 København K, Denmark, www.kb.dk.

Tchicai's correspondance, his notes, music cassettes and printed archival material can be consulted at the Jazzcentret, Center for Dansk Jazzhistorie, Kjellerups Torv 2 9000 Aalborg, Denmark, www.jazzcentret.dk. Its website is hosting the extended John Tchicai Discography as compiled by Erik Raben. Go to https://jazzcentret.dk/dansk-jazzkatalog and scroll down to 'John Tchicai discographien'.

Claira, France

www.ingramcontent.com/pod-product-compliance
Lightning Source LLC
LaVergne TN
LVHW041313200726
843509LV00009B/478